ROOTS
of the
RICH
and
FAMOUS

Robert Davenport

TAYLOR PUBLISHING COMPANY
Dallas, Texas

This book is dedicated to my parents,
Harry Augustus Davenport
and
Jean Yeager Davenport,
without whom I wouldn't have any ancestors.

Published by Taylor Publishing Company
1550 West Mockingbird Lane
Dallas, Texas 75235
www.taylorpub.com

Library of Congress Cataloging-in-Publication Data

Davenport, Robert (Robert R.)
    Roots of the rich and famous / Robert R. Davenport.
       p.   cm.
    ISBN 0-87833-217-0
    1. Celebrities—Biography—Miscellanea. 2. Celebrities—Genealogy.
I. Title.
CT105.D344   1998
920.073—dc21
[B]   98-38969
                                   CIP

Printed in the United States of America
10 9 8 7 6 5 4 3 2 1

CONTENTS

ACKNOWLEDGMENTS

A very big thanks to my agent, Jake Elwell, of Wieser and Wieser, without whom this book would not have been possible. Thanks also to Camille Cline, who acquired this book for Taylor, for seeing the book through to completion.

Special thanks to Amos Hanks (Tom Hanks), Lucy Arnaz, Ginger Rogers, Mrs. Lee Marvin, Robert Carradine, Ralph Edwards, Cesar Romero, Ernest Borgnine, Mrs. Robert King (Perry King), Jane Wyatt, Kerri Collins Perez (Bo Derek, John Derek), Sir N. Bayard Dill, Kt. (uncle of Michael Douglas), Sherri Harris (Elvis Presley), Rev. Kenneth O. Brown (Carradines), Stephen Peck (Gregory Peck), Robert Selleck (Tom Selleck), Mrs. Christopher B. Wyatt (Jane Wyatt), Joan Fontaine, Kenneth A. Bealer (Barbara Eden), David Crosby, Lillian Gish, Quincy Jones, Patrick Macnee, Harry Hollingsworth (Steve McQueen), Hugh Downs, John Lithgow, William Christopher, Gale Storm, Robert Duvall, Darell Brown of the Los Angeles Public Library, the Margaret Herrick Library of the Academy of Motion Picture Arts and Sciences, and of course my good friend, the world-famous genealogist Gary Boyd Roberts.

INTRODUCTION

Mark Twain once said, "My grandfather was cut down in the prime of his life. My grandmother always used to tell us that if he had been cut down fifteen minutes earlier, he could have been resuscitated."

Genealogy is the fastest-growing hobby in the country today. Although it was already a popular pastime when the miniseries *Roots* hit the scene, that show propelled the world's most fascinating hobby into America's most popular leisure-time activity.

Everyone has ancestors, and celebrities are no exception. And often the rich and famous have ancestors who were as well known as they are. Most celebrities today are creatures of the media, and so were their ancestors. Many historical figures are not famous so much for what they did as for the publicity that surrounded their exploits and enabled them to leave their permanent mark on historical record. For example, Davy Crockett not only led an interesting life, but he ensured his popularity by writing several best-selling books about himself. Even Pocahontas was hawking her wares, sent to England on a publicity tour to popularize tobacco, specifically because her reputation had preceded her. Therefore, it should come as no surprise that those historical figures who were good at self-promotion should be related to present-day celebrities.

Not only are famous persons related to other famous persons, but they are related to everyone else. If you dig deep enough into your own ancestry, you might find you are related to someone famous. And you might just find a famous ancestor, as well as something about yourself.

Photo Credits

Eddie Brandt: Bacall, Brynner, Dean, L. Dern, Disney, Eastwood, Edie, Fonda, Garland, Harlow, Harris, Hayworth, Karloff, King, Selleck, Temple, T. Williams

Dictionary of American Portraits: Arnold, Blair, Blount, D. Boone, G. Borden, L. Borden, J. Brown, N. Brown, Burr, Carson, Crockett, Cleveland, Franklin, Garfield, U. S. Grant, W. R. Hearst, Henry, Hickok, James, Kearny, J. F. Kennedy, Key, Lanier, L. H. H. Lee, R .E. Lee, Lincoln, Longfellow, Marshall, J. Monroe, Morton, J. Onassis, Paine, Pocahontas, Poe, T. Power 2nd, Revere, Rockefeller, Roosevelt, Rutledge, Sherman, Simpson, Stuyvesant, Taylor, Van Buren, Washington, Webster, Whitney, Whittier, W. Williams, E. B. Wilson, W. Wilson, Wright, Young, Younger

Sy Sussman: Arnaz, Autry, Bankhead, Basinger, Baxter, Bogart, Carillo, J. Carradine, Chase, Clift, Close, Coburn, Costner, Day-Lewis, De Mille, B. Dern, K. Douglas, M. Douglas, Farrow, Fitzgerald, Ford, Gish, Grahame, Hanks, Hardy, Hawn, P. Hearst, Hepburn, Holden, A. Huston, J. Huston, W. Huston, Jennings, Jones, Kelly, Lawford, Lombard, Lugosi, Marvin, Massey, McQueen, Mitchum, M. Monroe, O'Sullivan, Oxenberg, Perkins, T. Power, Presley, Price, Rathbone, Reynolds, Shields, Stewart, Sullavan, Tone, Tracy, Ustinov, J. Wayne, P. Wayne, Weld, T. Williams, Winters, Woodward, Wyatt

Auberjonois, courtesy Rene Auberjonois; P. Boone, court. Pat Boone; Borgia, ancient painting; Bush, court. the White House; R. Carradine, court. Robert Carradine; Christopher, courtesy of William Christopher; Davenport, court. Robert Davenport.; Dill, court. Sir Bayard Dill; Downs, court. Hugh Downs; Dracula, ancient painting; Eden, courtesy Barbara Eden fan club; R. Edwards, Gov. Edwards, court. Ralph Edwards; Hefner, court. Hugh Hefner; King, court. Perry King; Lithgow, court. John Lithgow; MacNee, court. Patrick MacNee; Marti, Romero, court. Cesar Romero; Newton, court. Wayne Newton; Quayle, court. White House; Prince Charles, Princess Diana, court. British Embassy, Los Angeles, California

One

HEIRLOOMS

Sometimes the best proof of your ancestry is an artifact you inherited that provides tangible evidence that you are descended from a famous ancestor. It's hard to throw away that lamp, no matter how horrible and tasteless, if it came over on the Mayflower!

William Christopher

WILLIAM CHRISTOPHER

William Christopher, who played Father Mulcahy on the long-running television series *M*A*S*H*, owns silverware that was handed down to him from his famous ancestor Paul Revere. As every grammar school student knows, Paul Revere made his immortal ride to tell the patriots that "the British are coming." What we didn't learn in school is that his preparation for the ride left something to be desired. Paul had forgotten his spurs, so he tied a note to his dog, who, like Lassie, ran home and returned shortly with the spurs tied around his neck. Paul had also forgotten padding, so he persuaded a young girl to give up her petticoat. History does not record exactly how he persuaded her, or exactly how long this delayed his famous ride!

PAUL REVERE

1

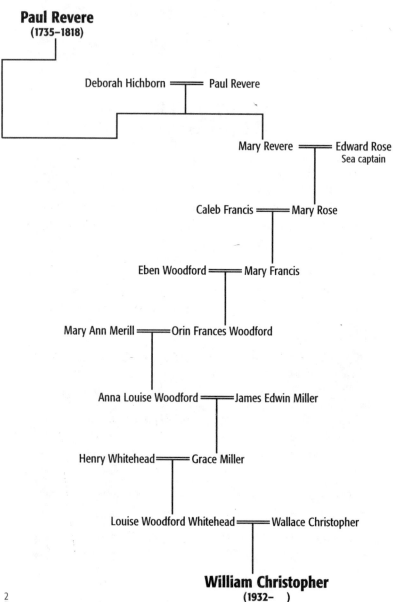

Paul Revere
(1735–1818)

Deborah Hichborn ═══ Paul Revere

Mary Revere ═══ Edward Rose
Sea captain

Caleb Francis ═══ Mary Rose

Eben Woodford ═══ Mary Francis

Mary Ann Merill ═══ Orin Frances Woodford

Anna Louise Woodford ═══ James Edwin Miller

Henry Whitehead ═══ Grace Miller

Louise Woodford Whitehead ═══ Wallace Christopher

William Christopher
(1932–)

Noteworthy: Former President George Bush is the son of senator Prescott Bush, whose first name memorialized his descent from Dr. Prescott, who completed the midnight ride after Paul Revere was captured by the British.

Lillian Gish

Film pioneer and Oscar-winning actress Lillian Gish proudly hung a painting of her cousin President Zachary Taylor in her living room to commemorate her relationship to the hero of the Mexican War, without whom the United States wouldn't have California or Hollywood.

LILLIAN GISH

Zachary Taylor almost didn't accept the nomination to be president while he was fighting in Mexico, because the letter sent to notify him arrived postage due, and he refused to accept it!

ZACHARY TAYLOR

Incumbent President James Polk, alarmed that he would lose the election to Taylor (who was winning battle after battle in Mexico), used dirty tricks that would make Nixon look like a choirboy. He reduced the size of Taylor's army, hoping he would be defeated in battle. However, Taylor still managed, although greatly outnumbered, to soundly defeat the Mexican general Santa Anna at the Battle of Buena Vista, and that victory swept him into the White House. As a point of interest, a street in Los Angeles named after that battle later became the home of Walt Disney Studios, and today various subdivisions of the company bear the name Buena Vista.

Noteworthy: Lillian Gish's ancestor, the Reverend Benjamin Gish, went west with the Reverend Jacob Eisenhower, the grandfather of President Dwight D. Eisenhower, and settled in Abilene, Texas.

Cesar Romero

Motion picture and television actor Cesar Romero is justly proud that he is the grandson of Jose Marti (1853-1895), the most famous figure of

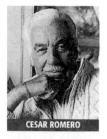
CESAR ROMERO

the Cubans in their struggle for independence from Spain, dubbed both "the Liberator" and "the George Washington of Cuba." Cesar inherited personal objects from Marti, including five of his oil paintings. Cesar's mother inherited the iron shackle with which Marti was imprisoned in Cuba, and in the 1950s she donated it to a museum. Cesar took an avid interest in Marti's life, and visited many of the locations where he spoke and worked among the Cuban revolutionaries, including places in Tampa, Florida, where he spoke to the Cuban refugee cigar makers.

Jose Marti was imprisoned by the Spanish because he wrote poems in support of the Cuban struggle for liberation from Spain. Released, he fled to New York City, where he met Carmen Mantilla, and the result of their union was Maria, Cesar's mother. Marti refused to allow her to attend school, insisting he teach her personally everything from reading French to math. Whenever he would leave on trips to raise funds for the Cuban revolution, Carmen would put her in school. When Marti returned, he would yank her out again, insisting that he was the only one who could give her a proper education. When he would give speeches in New York to Cuban revolu-

Cesar gave to the author this tintype of Marti and Maria, taken when she was a little girl.

tionaries, Maria would play the piano to entertain the men before the meetings. Marti carried Maria's picture with him constantly, over his heart, believing it would shield him from bullets. He returned to Cuba to fight in the revolution, and when, after his death, his body was recovered, they found Maria's picture over his heart, pierced by a bullet.

The legend of Marti lives on in Cuba. He is such an important national hero that when Russian premier Gorbachev visited Cuba, he and Fidel Castro laid a wreath on Marti's grave. The life story of Jose Marti was made into a feature film in Mexico, *La Rosa Blanca* (*The White Rose*), in 1953. Cesar Romero took his mother to this film, which was playing at a Spanish-language theater in Los Angeles, and she was impressed by the accuracy with which it portrayed Marti's life. In 1964 a statue of Marti on horseback was dedicated in New York City's Central Park, at the park entrance at 59th Street and the Avenue of the Americas.

Anjelica Huston

ANJELICA HUSTON

The Huston family has always worked together, starting when John Huston directed his father, Walter Huston, in *The Treasure of the Sierra Madre*. It came full circle with *The Dead*, for which John's son Tony Huston wrote the screenplay, and John directed his daughter Anjelica. Their working relationship had started when John directed her first film, *A Walk with Love*. Anjelica's memories of that movie, which were very painful, prevented them from working together for sixteen years. When they finally did rejoin, in *Prizzi's Honor*, she walked away with an Oscar, and he was nominated as best director.

When John Huston got his draft call for World War II, he was in the middle of directing Bogie in a scene in which the actor was surrounded by Japanese soldiers. Huston walked right off the set, saying, "Bogie can fight his own way out of this one." Huston's military tradition goes back to his maternal great-grandfather William Richardson, a general in the Civil War who

WALTER HUSTON

JOHN HUSTON

lost his arm at Chancellorsville and later became attorney general of Ohio. At the end of the war, General Richardson was given a sword by the men of the 25th Ohio, and John Huston could recite his acceptance speech by heart: "The value of this gift is immeasurably enhanced by the fact that it was given to me by men who have proven their valor in their country's cause on many a well-fought field. Wealth, influence, or favoritism might procure such a gift as this, but the esteem and confidence of brave men cannot be bought."

William Holden

At the 1939 World's Fair, William Holden was the guest of honor for "Golden Boy Day," named after the film that brought him to prominence. At a special ceremony on the steps of the Washington Hall pavilion, Messmore Kendall, president general of the Sons of the American Revolution, presented him with the coat of arms of the Washington family, which Holden subsequently hung in his office at Paramount. He was a relative of George

WILLIAM HOLDEN

Washington, through the Ball family, and the mothers of both George Washington and William Holden were named Mary Ball.

At the beginning of the Revolutionary War, Washington sent one of his officers to requisition horses from the local landowners. At one old country mansion, the lady of the house demanded to know on whose authority they came to take her horses. "On the orders of General George Washington, commander in chief of the American army," was the reply. Mary Ball smiled, and said, "You go tell the commander in chief of the American army that his mother says he cannot have her horses."

Perry King

PERRY KING

Actor Perry King, whose credits include the television series *Riptide*, has a number of interesting family heirlooms, including a cavalry saber that came from a royalist ancestor in the Revolution. King's mother also has a silver cup that belonged to Lord Howe, the commander of the British forces in the Revolution, who was also a relative, and who had visited his American cousins during the war. Howe felt badly about the Revolution, and always hoped that America would come back into the empire.

There is still a sword in the family on which is inscribed, "Edmund Perkins, Gent.," that was handed down from an ancestor who arrived in America in the 1600s. King's ancestor James Perkins had a fleet of clipper ships that was in the business of running opium to China. He made so much money as a drug dealer that he was able to donate the money to found Perkins Institute for the Blind.

ROGER SHERMAN

Perry King is also descended from two signers of the Declaration of Independence, Roger Sherman and John Morton. Roger Sherman was the only man to sign the Declaration of Independence, the Articles of Confederation, and the U.S. Constitution. John Morton, a signer of the Declaration from Pennsylvania, was sent with the express purpose of voting against independence, and he was only persuaded to change his vote on July 1, 1776. On his return home Morton learned that all of his friends and family hated him for signing. He became so depressed that he died. On his deathbed his last words were, "Tell them they will live to see the day when they shall acknowledge that my signing the Declaration of Independence was the most glorious thing to ever happen in this family."

JOHN MORTON

Two

WHAT'S IN A NAME?

Parents often look to their ancestors for inspiration when choosing first names for their offspring. When they do, they affirm their family history, establishing for all the world to see that they are descended from a well-known historical figure. The following are some examples of famous people whose names honor their famous ancestry.

Desi Arnaz

DESI ARNAZ

Bandleader and TV star Desi Arnaz's great-great-grandmother Ventura was the lady after whom Ventura County in Southern California was named. His ancestors were not only influential citizens in California, but also in Cuba before the communist takeover. His father was the mayor of Santiago, Cuba. His mother, Dolores de Acha, was the daughter of one of the founders of the Bacardi Rum Company. His grandfather Don Desiderio Arnaz, after whom Desi was named, was Teddy Roosevelt's doctor and charged with the Rough Riders up San Juan Hill during the Spanish-American War in 1898.

Lauren Bacall

LAUREN BACALL

Actress Lauren Bacall was married to Humphrey Bogart, and when he died she placed a small gold whistle in his urn that was inscribed, "If you want anything, just whistle." This was her line to him in their first film together, *To Have and Have Not*.

Lauren Bacall, whose real last name is Persky, shares her last name with her first cousin, former Israeli prime minister Shimon Peres (born Persky). Born in Poland, Peres was an early immigrant to Israel, where he rose quickly to become the defense minister of the struggling country, shrewdly negotiating a treaty with France that guaranteed Israel a steady supply of arms and munitions. He built up Israel's military and then advocated a treaty in which the Sinai was returned to Egypt in return for a permanent peace between the two countries.

Tallulah Bankhead

Actress Tallulah Bankhead was named after her grandmother Tallulah J. Brockman, who was conceived at a stopover at Tallulah Falls, Georgia, when her parents were moving from South Carolina to Alabama. The original Tallulah, after whom the waterfall in Georgia was named, was a Choctaw princess.

Pat Boone

PAT BOONE

Popular singer and entertainer Pat Boone and actor Richard Boone are both related to the great frontiersman and Indian fighter Daniel Boone.

Unlike the way that Daniel is popularly portrayed, he never wore a coonskin cap, which was more Davy Crockett's style. Boone, in the days before the Revolution, brought settlers into the new territory of Kentucky, founding the fort at Boonesboro. However, he was not successful as a

DANIEL BOONE

businessman, and later settlers were able to obtain the land grants to the frontier he had forged from the wilderness. In disgust, he kept moving west, traveling as far as Yellowstone. An expert wood carver, he made his own coffin, which he kept under his bed.

KIT CARSON

KIT CARSON

Frontiersman and Indian scout Christopher "Kit" Carson would not have been born in America had it not been for an ancestor of Daniel Boone. Carson's great-grandfather, the Reverend Alexander Carson, a Presbyterian minister, was a friend of George Boone, the grandfather of Daniel Boone, in England. Excited by reports from his sons, Squire Boone and George Boone, who had already immigrated to Pennsylvania, both George Boone Sr. and the Reverend Carson were persuaded to immigrate together to America.

Kit Carson gained his greatest fame as Frémont's scout, and during the Mexican War was instrumental in the capture of San Diego and Los Angeles. Later he was the first to bring the news of the California gold strike back east. He continued to serve as a scout and to fight Indians, and during the Civil War he became a general and fought against the Kiowa and Comanche tribes. In recognition of his contribution to the settlement of the West, the capital city of Nevada was named after him.

Cubby Broccoli

Producer Cubby Broccoli, the genius behind the James Bond movies, claims descent from the family who created the vegetable broccoli. It was originally developed by the Broccoli family of Carrera, Italy, who crossed cauliflower and rabe, and then Cubby's uncle introduced broccoli into the United States.

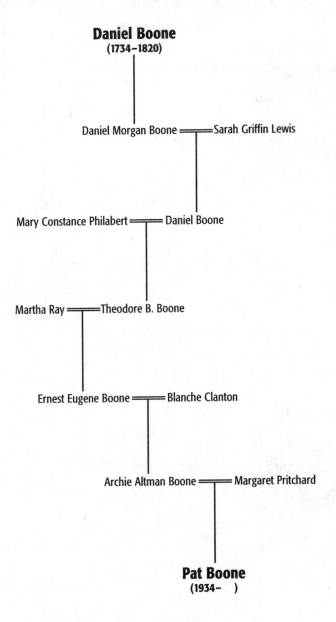

Daniel Boone
(1734–1820)

Daniel Morgan Boone ===== Sarah Griffin Lewis

Mary Constance Philabert ===== Daniel Boone

Martha Ray ===== Theodore B. Boone

Ernest Eugene Boone ===== Blanche Clanton

Archie Altman Boone ===== Margaret Pritchard

Pat Boone
(1934–   )

F. Scott Fitzgerald

F. SCOTT FITZGERALD

Perhaps one of the best examples of a person whose famous ancestor is clearly identified in his own name is author F. Scott Fitzgerald. Because of his relationship to Francis Scott Key, his mother gave him the "Star Spangled" name of Francis Scott Key Fitzgerald, which he shortened to F. Scott.

During the British bombardment of Fort McHenry in the War of 1812, Francis Scott Key had written a rough draft of "The Star Spangled Banner" on the back of a letter he had in his pocket. In less than an hour the words had made their way all over town. The newspapers immediately took it up and spread it all over the country. The poem, still without a tune, was circulated throughout the army to raise the morale of the troops. Two soldiers then added a tune that fit the words.

FRANCIS SCOTT KEY

It is said that Key did not know one tune from another. Once, in Tuscaloosa, Alabama, a reception was given in his honor, at which the orchestra played "The Star Spangled Banner." To everyone's surprise, Key complimented the music, not recognizing the song as his own!

Jane Fonda

JANE FONDA

Actress Jane Fonda's mother, Frances Seymour, claims a relationship to Jane Seymour, who was the third of the six wives of Henry VIII. For the first years of Jane's life, Frances Fonda called her daughter "Lady Jane." Her mother was no historian: she confused her ancestor with the nine-day queen of England, Lady Jane Grey.

Jane Seymour came to the attention of Henry VIII when he was still married to Anne Boleyn. In fact Queen Anne had a miscarriage in her agitation over the king's lust for Jane. However, Jane

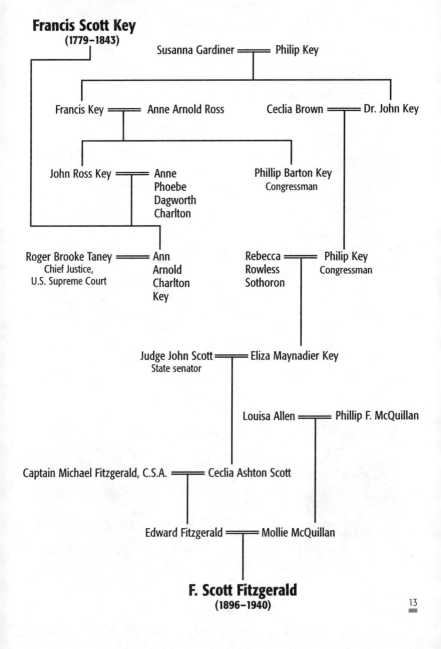

Francis Scott Key
(1779–1843)

Susanna Gardiner ═══ Philip Key

Francis Key ═══ Anne Arnold Ross

Ceclia Brown ═══ Dr. John Key

John Ross Key ═══ Anne Phoebe Dagworth Charlton

Phillip Barton Key
Congressman

Roger Brooke Taney ═══ Ann Arnold Charlton Key
Chief Justice,
U.S. Supreme Court

Rebecca Rowless Sothoron ═══ Philip Key
Congressman

Judge John Scott ═══ Eliza Maynadier Key
State senator

Louisa Allen ═══ Phillip F. McQuillan

Captain Michael Fitzgerald, C.S.A. ═══ Ceclia Ashton Scott

Edward Fitzgerald ═══ Mollie McQuillan

F. Scott Fitzgerald
(1896–1940)

refused his advances, insisting that "he wouldn't get a thing until she got the ring." This prompted Henry to devise a scheme whereby he accused Queen Anne of adultery, which allowed him to then cut off her head. After what he deemed a suitable period of mourning—three days—he gave Jane that ring.

Oliver Hardy

OLIVER HARDY

Oliver Hardy, the weightier side of the comedy team of Laurel and Hardy, was the son of Oliver Hardy, a lawyer from England who claimed descent from Vice Admiral Sir Thomas Hardy. Sir Thomas was the close friend and aide-de-camp to Admiral Horatio Nelson, who was the hero of the battle of Trafalgar during the Napoleonic Wars and the commander during that battle of the *HMS Victory*. The victory at Trafalgar was so great that it gave Britannia undisputed command of the world's seas for more than a century. As Nelson lay dying, he called many times for his friend Hardy, who could not leave his command during the battle. After victory seemed inevitable, Hardy was able to go below to see his friend. Nelson gave him instructions on his personal affairs, and his final request was, "Kiss me, Hardy." This bulldog of the sea knelt down and gave Nelson a kiss on the forehead. Nelson said, "Thank God I have done my duty," and died.

Tyrone Power

TYRONE POWER

Actor Tyrone Power, in his time known as the king of Twentieth Century-Fox, was descended from a long line of actors. His first ancestor in America, who died in 1798, was also named Tyrone Power. That Power's son, the second Tyrone Power, was an actor and playwright who drowned on the steamship

TYRONE POWER, 2nd

President returning from Europe in 1841. Tyrone Jr.'s son was on the stage under the name Harold Page, and Harold's son, the third Tyrone Power, was a highly acclaimed stage actor who died in Los Angeles in 1931, after making his first talking picture. The fourth Tyrone Power is the world famous film star. His son, the fifth Tyrone Power, is also an actor.

Norman Rockwell

Norman Rockwell, the great twentieth-century painter whose work invariably graced the cover of the *Saturday Evening Post* and *Boy's Life*, descended from the knight Sir Norman Percevel, and his mother was so proud of this ancestor that she named him Norman Percevel Rockwell. Sir Norman's claim to fame occurred when he kicked Guy Fawkes down the stairs of the Tower of London after Fawkes tried to blow up the House of Lords on November 4, 1605. The British find the anniversary of this infamous "gunpowder plot" a good excuse for their annual fireworks, since they cannot in good conscience set them off on the Fourth of July.

Norman Rockwell is also related to Alfonso Rockwell, the inventor of the electric chair. After the Civil War, Dr. Rockwell had attended a number of hangings in which the rope broke, and the luckless miscreants had to be hanged a second time. While such bungling was great entertainment, he wanted to create a more humane way to dispose of undesirable citizens.

Norman Schwarzkopf

General Norman Schwarzkopf Jr., of Gulf War fame, has been described as "a cross between Willard Scott, Jonathan Winters, and Attila the Hun." The hero of the Gulf War is the son of General Norman Schwarzkopf Sr., who distinguished himself as a chief of police in charge of the investigation surrounding the kidnapping and murder of Charles A. Lindberg's infant son. Norman Sr. was able to prove that the kidnappers had accidentally killed the boy while trying to climb down the ladder with the baby on the night of the kidnapping. His fame led to his becoming the host of the popular *Gangbusters* radio program. He later went on to become an intelligence officer in the U.S. Army in World War II and mastermind the countercoup that restored the Shah to the Iranian throne in 1954.

Steven Spielberg

Film director Steven Spielberg's ancestors are portrayed with some accuracy in his animated film *An American Tail*, which chronicles the adventures of a Jewish mouse named Fievel coming to America. Spielberg made this film shortly after his own ancestry was researched, and he was very influenced in Fievel's creation by the revelations about his ancestors. His grandfather, upon whom the film was based, immigrated to this country from Russia and was named Fievel.

John Washington

Actor John Augustine Washington V played his ancestor John Augustine Washington (the brother of George Washington) in the television miniseries *Washington,* which starred Barry Bostwick.

Michael Wilding

Actor Michael Wilding, best known today as the second husband of Elizabeth Taylor, was the number-one idol of the British cinema in the late 1940s. He was a direct descendant of the archbishop of Canterbury who crowned Queen Victoria, as well as a descendant of John of Gaunt, which is why his middle name is "Gauntlet." Michael Wilding was once asked whether there was anything about actors that made them different from other people. He replied, "Without a doubt. You can always pick out an actor by the glazed look that comes into his eyes when the conversation wanders away from himself."

Richard Zanuck

Film producer Richard Zanuck, whose credits include *Cocoon* and *Driving Miss Daisy,* is the son of former Twentieth Century-Fox head of production Darryl Zanuck, whose grandfather Henry Turpin claimed they were direct descendants of the legendary English highwayman Dick Turpin.

Dick Turpin, mounted on his famous horse, Black Bess, rode up and down the Great North Road in England, robbing the rich passengers of the Royal Mail coaches of their money and jewels. He originally worked with a gang, selecting lonely farmhouses where he knew the men were away and then torturing the defenseless women into yielding their valuables. This sort of thing wasn't really considered good form, and with a reward of two hundred guineas on each of their heads, it wasn't long before two members of the gang were swinging from the gallows.

Dick thought it advisable to get a new partner, and he entered into a profitable arrangement with highwayman Tom King. When the law caught up with Tom at an inn, Dick bravely rode up to save him, fired his pistol, missed the policeman, and shot Tom. Tom was not pleased, and before he died proceeded to give the authorities complete details on where to find Dick. After that, he worked alone, probably because partners are hard to find after you shoot one. He was ultimately arrested and hanged for horse stealing.

Bill Clinton

President William Jefferson Clinton has not inherited too many traits from his great-great-grandfather, Thomas Jefferson Blythe. Blythe was convicted of gambling in 1850, after betting on the outcome of a sheriff's political race. However, even though he was a convicted criminal, Thomas did not try to evade his military service like his more famous descendant, fighting for three years in the Confederate army in the 34th Mississippi Infantry.

Three

U.S. PRESIDENTS

◎◎

Tom Hanks	≋ Abraham Lincoln
Quincy Jones	≋ George Washington
Chet Huntley	≋ John Adams
The Carradines	≋ James Monroe
T. S. Eliot	≋ John Quincy Adams
Glenn Ford	≋ Martin Van Buren
Ginger Rogers	≋ George Washington
William Holden	≋ George Washington
Lillian and Dorothy Gish	≋ Zachary Taylor
Elvis Presley	≋ Abraham Lincoln
Judy Garland	≋ Ulysses S. Grant
Glenn Close	≋ Grover Cleveland
Robert Hays	≋ William Henry Harrison
Gore Vidal	≋ William McKinley
John Lithgow	≋ James A. Garfield
Bill Cosby	≋ Abraham Lincoln
Nelson Eddy	≋ Martin Van Buren
Orson Bean	≋ Calvin Coolidge
Randolph Scott	≋ James Madison

Quincy Jones

In my conversations with world-famous musician Quincy Jones, I discovered that he is more proud of the fact that his ancestry goes back to a long line of famous musicians than of his relationship to President George Washington. His ancestor John Lanier was the court musician to Henry VIII, king of England. Nicholas Lanier, his brother, was musician to Queen

QUINCY JONES

SIDNEY LANIER

Elizabeth I. Nicholas had ten children, all of whom were musicians in the service of the crown. Even more distinguished was Nicholas Lanier, the son of John, who held a high position among the court musicians in the royal household as both a composer and performer and was proclaimed "musician of the flutes" in 1604. The Lanier family became, upon their arrival in Virginia, a prominent and influential family of the South. Other relatives of Quincy Jones include the poet Sidney Lanier and playwright Tennessee Williams.

With such talent in his background, it is no surprise that Quincy Jones has made such an impression on the music world, from writing the music for *Roots* and *The Color Purple* to producing Michael Jackson's hit album *Thriller,* among others.

GEORGE WASHINGTON

Ginger Rogers

In my communications with actress Ginger Rogers, she talked about her maternal grandmother, Saphrona Ball, who was a descendant of Mary Ball Washington, George Washington's mother. On her father's side, Ginger was admitted to the Daughters of the American Revolution based on her descent from James McGrath, a Revolutionary War soldier from Pennsylvania.

Ginger's father was the great-grandson of Dr. John Sappington, who introduced the use of quinine pills to ward off malaria. Sappington first sold this formula from the back of a wagon, then later set up a practice in Arrow Rock, Missouri. He had a knack for siring beautiful daughters, and his daughter Jane was married to Claiborne F. Jackson, the governor of Missouri during the Civil War. When Jane died, the governor married her sister Louisa. When Louisa in turn expired, Dr. Sappington didn't seem to think it unusual for Claiborne to marry his third daughter, Eliza. For some

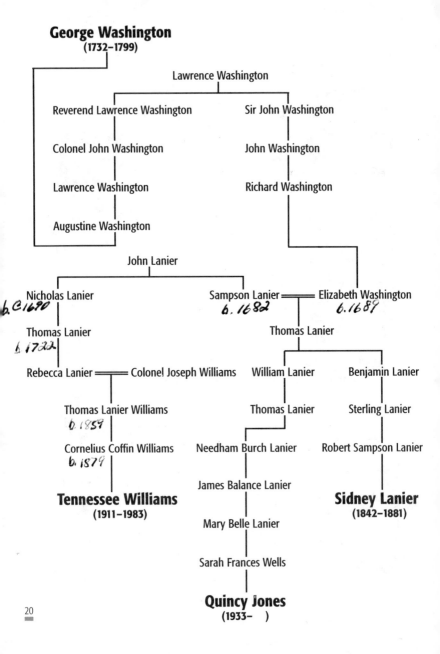

George Washington
(1732–1799)

Lawrence Washington

Reverend Lawrence Washington

Sir John Washington

Colonel John Washington

John Washington

Lawrence Washington

Richard Washington

Augustine Washington

John Lanier

Nicholas Lanier
b. c 1690

Sampson Lanier
b. 1682

Elizabeth Washington
b. 1689

Thomas Lanier
b. 1722

Thomas Lanier

Rebecca Lanier ═══ Colonel Joseph Williams

William Lanier

Benjamin Lanier

Thomas Lanier Williams
b. 1859

Thomas Lanier

Sterling Lanier

Cornelius Coffin Williams
b. 1879

Needham Burch Lanier

Robert Sampson Lanier

Tennessee Williams
(1911–1983)

James Balance Lanier

Sidney Lanier
(1842–1881)

Mary Belle Lanier

Sarah Frances Wells

Quincy Jones
(1933–   )

reason neither the father nor the daughter were wary of the fate that had befallen her two sisters. Dr. Jackson's only remark on the subject was that now that Claiborne had all of his daughters, he better not come back for his wife!

Chet Huntley

Newscaster Chet Huntley is a descendant of John Adams, the political firebrand of the American Revolution. During his two terms as vice president, Adams became firmly convinced that George Washington was going to outlive him and would remain in office as long as it took to ensure that he would never make it to the top spot.

The Carradines

ROBERT CARRADINE

The acting Carradines are related to President James Monroe, famous for the Monroe Doctrine.

Robert Carradine, Keith Carradine, and David Carradine are all sons of famous character actor John Carradine, and Keith is the father of actress Martha Plimpton. According to Keith, the family tree is pretty com-

JOHN CARRADINE

plicated. He shares a common mother and father with Robert Carradine, he and David have only their father in common, and with actor Michael Bowen he has only a mother in common.

JAMES MONROE

John Carradine's great-grandfather was Dr. Beverly Carradine, a freelance evangelist who toured the country preaching in churches, tents, and camp meetings. He became a household name among Methodists and those known as the "holiness movement." A branch of this movement later became known as the Holy Rollers, although Dr. Carradine always disavowed any connection with them because he did not believe in speaking in tongues, handling snakes, or divine healing.

Elvis Presley

ELVIS PRESLEY

Elvis Presley, the King of Rock and Roll, made his motion picture debut in a period film, *Love Me Tender*, set during the administration of his relative Abraham Lincoln.

Elvis also had an interesting connection to actress and talk show host Oprah Winfrey. Her third great-grandfather, Lewis Presley, was a cousin of Andrew Presley Jr. (born 1754), the fourth great-grandfather of Elvis Presley. Their families grew up in towns less than one hun-

ABRAHAM LINCOLN

dred miles apart in Mississippi. Elvis was from Tupelo, Oprah from Kosciusko. They are both direct descendants of John Presley, who emigrated from Scotland to America in 1745.

Noteworthy: Abe's son Robert Todd Lincoln is connected to every president who has been assassinated. He accompanied his father to the house across the street from Ford's Theatre where he died. In 1881 Robert, then secretary of war to Garfield, went to the railroad station to meet the president, only to see him shot. Twenty years later he was invited by McKinley to meet him at the Pan American Exposition in Buffalo, New York, and arrived just in time to see him shot. After that, Robert avoided presidents, declaring, "There is a certain fatality about presidential functions when I am present." He could not escape, however; he is buried in Arlington National Cemetery along with president John F. Kennedy!

Tom Hanks

In 1989 Oscar-winning actor Tom Hank's father, Amos Hanks, visited Malmesbury, England, on a genealogical hunt. Malmesbury, where Hankses outnumber Joneses and Smiths, has been the ancestral seat of the Hanks family since A.D. 940. Through his diligent research (which he shared with the author), Amos was able to establish their relationship to Nancy Hanks, the mother of Abraham Lincoln.

TOM HANKS

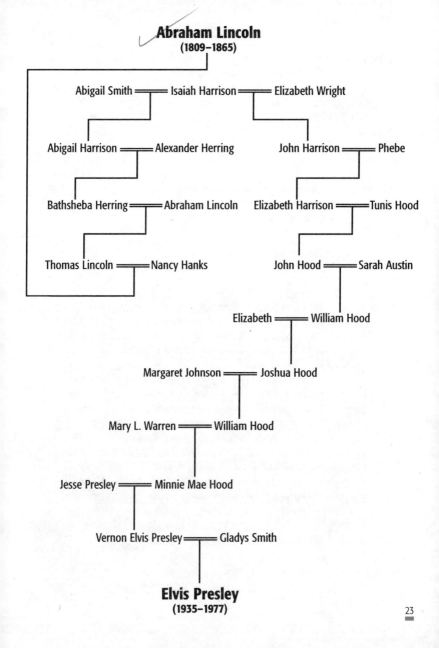

Abraham Lincoln
(1809–1865)

Abigail Smith ══ Isaiah Harrison ══ Elizabeth Wright

Abigail Harrison ══ Alexander Herring

John Harrison ══ Phebe

Bathsheba Herring ══ Abraham Lincoln

Elizabeth Harrison ══ Tunis Hood

Thomas Lincoln ══ Nancy Hanks

John Hood ══ Sarah Austin

Elizabeth ══ William Hood

Margaret Johnson ══ Joshua Hood

Mary L. Warren ══ William Hood

Jesse Presley ══ Minnie Mae Hood

Vernon Elvis Presley ══ Gladys Smith

Elvis Presley
(1935–1977)

Comedy must be a powerful gene in the Hanks family, serving both Tom and Abe well. Of all of our presidents, Lincoln was one of the best writers, and there is no doubt that he was the funniest. Once, when walking into town, Lincoln hailed a man driving by and asked him if he would take his coat into town. When he agreed, Lincoln then added, "Can I ride inside my coat?"

Lincoln ordered the end of the draft when the war ended. That evening he went to a play, in which a lady asks for a shawl to stop a chilly draft. Improvising, the actor said, "The president has already stopped the draft." This was Lincoln's last laugh. He was watching *Our American Cousin*, and minutes later he was shot.

BILL COSBY

Comedian Bill Cosby's wife, Camille Hanks, is descended from the same Hanks family as actor Tom Hanks, and Nancy Hanks, who was the mother of Abraham Lincoln. Bill is so proud of his wife's ancestry that on *The Cosby Show* he used Hanks as the maiden name of his TV wife, Claire Huxtable.

Bill Cosby's own ancestry is a good example of a typical African-American family in America. At the end of the Civil War, most slaves adopted surnames for the first time. They normally used the name of either a famous American, such as a president, or, as in the case of Bill Cosby, the surname of the person who owned them at the time they were born. When plantation owner John Cosby died in 1829, his will mentioned his slave Maria and her son Sam. Sam Cosby got the family off to a good start after the Civil War, because unlike the majority of freed slaves, who were field hands, he was a skilled artisan, a blacksmith. They lived in Schuyler, Nelson County, Virginia, about twenty miles from Charlottesville. Schuyler is better known today as Walton's Mountain, the setting of the long-running television series *The Waltons*.

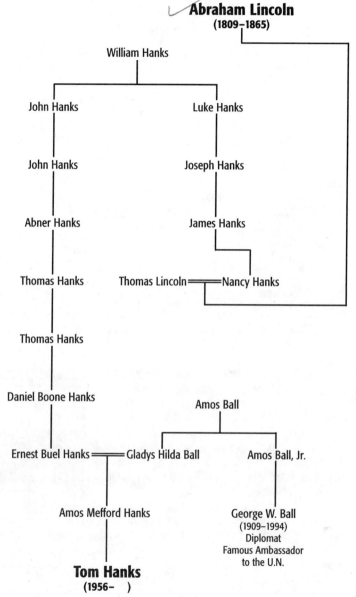

Abraham Lincoln
(1809–1865)

William Hanks

John Hanks

Luke Hanks

John Hanks

Joseph Hanks

Abner Hanks

James Hanks

Thomas Hanks

Thomas Lincoln══Nancy Hanks

Thomas Hanks

Daniel Boone Hanks

Amos Ball

Ernest Buel Hanks══Gladys Hilda Ball

Amos Ball, Jr.

Amos Mefford Hanks

George W. Ball
(1909–1994)
Diplomat
Famous Ambassador
to the U.N.

Tom Hanks
(1956–   )

T. S. Eliot

Author T. S. Eliot, known to history as the voice of a disillusioned generation, was related to President John Quincy Adams. He is today famous as the author of *Old Possum's Book of Practical Cats*, a book of verse for children he wrote in 1939, which became the basis for the Broadway musical *Cats*. Eliot was a connoisseur of words, a poet, critic, and playwright, but few knew of his mania for cheese. He made this quite clear when he announced, "I find I can no longer travel except where there is an excellent native cheese."

Glenn Ford

GLENN FORD

Actor Glenn Ford radiated integrity and determination and was invariably the "good guy." He claims to be a descendant of Martin Van Buren, the eighth president.

When Van Buren ran for president, his party used his nickname, "Old Kinderhook," after the town where he was born, as the name for the Old Kinderhook Club reelection committee, coining a new expression in the English language with their rallying cry, "Van Buren is O.K."

Congressman and frontier wit Davy Crockett had a low opinion of the president: "Van Buren is what the English call a dandy. When he enters the senate in the morning, he struts and swaggers like a crow. He is laced up in corsets, such as women in town wear, and, if possible, tighter than the best of them. It would be difficult to say, from his personal appearance, whether he was a man or woman, but for large whiskers."

MARTIN VAN BUREN

Van Buren was so hated in the South that in the 1848 campaign he only received nine votes there, all of them from Virginia. His supporters cried, "Fraud!" prompting a Virginian to state: "It's a fraud, all right. We're still looking for the son-of-a-b—— who voted nine times."

Judy Garland

JUDY GARLAND

Actress Judy Garland and her first cousin, U.S. Grant, have in common their hereditary problems with substance abuse. They didn't have musical talent in common, however. General Grant claimed that he knew only two tunes, one was "Yankee Doodle," and the other wasn't.

After the Mexican War, Grant was thrown out of the army because of his drinking, and he was a total failure in civilian life. He peddled firewood, tried to sell real estate, and his store went bankrupt. The Civil War was his salvation. Many people complained to Lincoln that Grant was a habitual drunk. Lincoln's reply: "This man wins battles. Find out what brand he drinks, and send a case to each of my generals."

U. S. GRANT

Both Grant and Garland had a good sense of humor. When Judy was on *The Tonight Show*, Jack Paar asked her if a certain actress was a nymphomaniac. Judy replied, "Only if you can calm her down." Grant once entered an inn in the middle of a storm, looking pretty much the worse for wear. A number of lawyers were clustered by the fire, and one remarked, "You look like you've been through hell. How was it?" "Just like here," retorted Grant, "All the lawyers were near the fire."

Glenn Close

GLENN CLOSE

Actress Glenn Close is related to Grover Cleveland, who, although he was president, is not the namesake for the city in Ohio. That distinction goes to their cousin General Moses Cleaveland, who led the first surveying party into the wilds of Ohio.

When Grover Cleveland was running for president, his opponents taunted him with the line, "Ma, ma, where's my pa? Gone to the White House, ha, ha, ha." They tried to make a campaign issue out of his illegitimate daughter. But Cleveland's advice to his campaign managers, obviously lost on later generations of presidents, was, "Whatever we say, it better be the truth."

GROVER CLEVELAND

Noteworthy: His daughter Ruth gave her name to the Baby Ruth candy bar.

Robert Hays

Actor Robert Hays, best known for the film *Airplane!*, is related to both the presidents Harrison.

' Villiam Henry Harrison's presidential campaign featured a huge paper ball that was rolled from Kentucky to the presidential convention in Baltimore, which gave us the expression "keep the ball rolling." Harrison caught pneumonia at his own inauguration, reading a speech written for him by Daniel Webster, and died one month later, becoming the first president to die in office. As Ralph Waldo Emerson said, "He could not stand the excitement of seventeen million people adoring him, and died of the presidency in one month." Benjamin Harrison, grandson of William Henry Harrison, was also president.

John Adams said of Benjamin's great-grandfather and namesake, who signed the Declaration of Independence, "Harrison was an indolent, luxurious, heavy gentleman, of no use in Congress or committee, but a great embarrassment to both." He was also a dirty old man. His first wife, Caroline Lavinia Scott, became ill, and she invited her niece, Mary Scott Lord, to come to the White House to help take over some of the burden of running the house. Mary was the same age as Harrison's daughter Mamie. It is not known exactly all of the duties that Mary assumed, but after the death of Caroline, Harrison married her!

Gore Vidal

Author Gore Vidal claims as a relative President William McKinley, whom he treats at length in his book *Empire*. When McKinley visited Niagara Falls as president, he only went halfway across because he didn't want to be the first president to leave the United States while in office. McKinley was one of the four presidents who were assassinated, being shot by a young anarchist named Leon Czolgosz, who waited patiently in a receiving line at the Pan American Exhibition in Buffalo to shake his hand. When Czolgosz got to the head of the line, he shot McKinley. Justice was swift back then, and Czolgosz was electrocuted forty-five days later.

A friend once showed Gore Vidal a number of pictures taken of him at an international writers conference, and each picture showed him sitting next to an Indian delegate. "I always sit next to a man in a turban," he explained. "You get photographed more."

John Lithgow

JOHN LITHGOW

After the author told film and television star John Lithgow that he was related to president James Garfield, Lithgow responded with a note that said, "When I learned that I was related to Garfield, I toasted him all night!"

Garfield was shot while in office, and if it had not been for his medical treatment he would have lived. He was able to survive the doctors for eleven weeks, be-fore their assistance finally killed him. The bullet was lodged in his body, and the doctors were deter-mined to find it. Although they knew the bullet would cause infection, they neglected to sterilize their fingers and instruments. They poked around for days. One doctor even got his probe stuck in one of Garfield's shattered ribs, and it was only with great pain to the president that he yanked it out.

JAMES GARFIELD

They even brought in Alexander Graham Bell, who had invented a de-vice similar to a mine detector, to try to find the bullet. Observing the qual-ity of his medical attention, Garfield declared, "I am a dead man." He was right.

JOHN F. KENNEDY

JFK's first marriage was a well-kept secret, hidden by the money his father, former ambassador to England Joseph P. Kennedy, threw at the problem. The elder Kennedy knew that in 1960 a divorced man would have no chance at the presidency. The first wife of John F. Kennedy was Malcom Durie, who was herself already twice divorced, from Firmin Desolge IV and F. John Bersbach. It is doubtful that even Jacqueline Bouvier, Jack's second wife, knew about his first wife.

JOHN F. KENNEDY

JACKIE ONASSIS

JACKIE ONASSIS

Former First Lady Jacqueline Lee Bouvier, who made headlines when she married billionaire Aristotle Onassis after the early death of her husband, President John F. Kennedy, is descended from a soldier in Napoleon's army, Michel Bouvier. Having fought with the emperor during his many campaigns to conquer Europe, Michel rallied to him once again during the famous Hundred Days, when Napoleon made his final bid to regain his throne. Finally defeated at the Battle of Waterloo, Napoleon was forced to abdicate. The new king of France, Louis XVIII, placed in power by the victorious allies, immediately announced that anyone who had joined Napoleon was subject to execution. Michel Bouvier didn't wait to test the legality of this decree—he immediately boarded a ship for New York.

Four

HORROR

Actors who are masters of horror mix with real-life horrors in this chapter! Bela Lugosi made his mark on film by portraying one of Prince Charles's most infamous ancestors, but Lon Chaney and Boris Karloff brought their ghouls to life without role models!
☺☺

Prince Charles

Prince Charles is descended from Voivode Vlad Dracula. Known to his friends as Vlad the Impaler, Dracula was an interesting historical figure. When the bloodthirsty Turks invaded his country they were shocked by the sight of thousands of his subjects impaled on stakes in the path of their invasion. This sight caused them to bypass Transylvania (today Hungary), fearful of what Dracula might do to an invader if he treated his own subjects in such a

PRINCE CHARLES

bloody fashion. Vlad Dracula the Impaler was finally killed by his own people, but not before he had engaged in a bloodbath that ended in the impaling of hundreds of thousands, thus enshrining in history the connection between blood and Count Dracula.

Although Bram Stoker's *Dracula*, published in London in 1897, gave the story new life, Dracula has been a popular pop figure for centuries. In

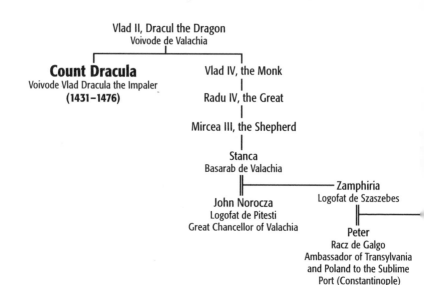

Vlad II, Dracul the Dragon
Voivode de Valachia

Count Dracula
Voivode Vlad Dracula the Impaler
(1431–1476)

Vlad IV, the Monk

Radu IV, the Great

Mircea III, the Shepherd

Stanca
Basarab de Valachia

John Norocza
Logofat de Pitesti
Great Chancellor of Valachia

Zamphiria
Logofat de Szaszebes

Peter
Racz de Galgo
Ambassador of Transylvania
and Poland to the Sublime
Port (Constantinople)

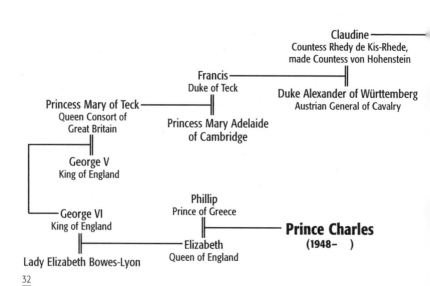

Claudine
Countess Rhedy de Kis-Rhede,
made Countess von Hohenstein

Francis
Duke of Teck

Duke Alexander of Württemberg
Austrian General of Cavalry

Princess Mary of Teck
Queen Consort of
Great Britain

Princess Mary Adelaide
of Cambridge

George V
King of England

Phillip
Prince of Greece

George VI
King of England

Prince Charles
(1948–   )

Elizabeth
Queen of England

Lady Elizabeth Bowes-Lyon

32

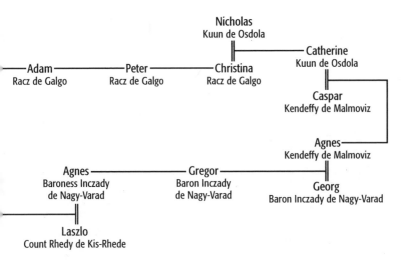

Nicholas
Kuun de Osdola

Catherine
Kuun de Osdola

Adam
Racz de Galgo

Peter
Racz de Galgo

Christina
Racz de Galgo

Caspar
Kendeffy de Malmoviz

Agnes
Kendeffy de Malmoviz

Agnes
Baroness Inczady
de Nagy-Varad

Gregor
Baron Inczady
de Nagy-Varad

Georg
Baron Inczady de Nagy-Varad

Laszlo
Count Rhedy de Kis-Rhede

1492 the top-selling stories were those published by Christopher Columbus about his trip to the New World and anything about Dracula.

Dracula once invited all of the nobles to a great feast and asked each of them if they could name the previous rulers of Transylvania. When none of them could, he had all 500 of them impaled and then sat down to finish his meal, watching the stakes slowly make their way through each of his victims. The bodies were then decapitated and fed to crabs, and the crabs were then served at a feast given by Dracula for the friends and relations of the murdered nobles. He certainly knew how to throw a party!

The savagery of Dracula knew few bounds, and he was always trying to be more creative. He had mothers eat their own children and husbands eat their wives. He impaled people right-side-up, upside-down, and sideways, the last manner allowing him to separately impale different parts of their bodies on different stakes. One writer, on approaching Dracula's castle, thought at first it was surrounded by a forest, but on getting closer he realized that the "trees" were thousands of persons impaled on stakes.

Impaling was not Dracula's only amusement. He once had a large copper kettle made with holes the size of heads in the lid. He would place people in the cauldron and bring it to a boil. The people would stick their heads through the holes and scream in agony as they were cooked to death.

Dracula was also a social reformer. Realizing that the plight of the homeless was an important problem in his country, he had all of the homeless people invited to a huge feast in a specially prepared building. They were then fed until they could barely move, at which point Dracula had the doors closed and the building burned down, thus "eliminating" the problem.

VLAD DRACULA

Bela Lugosi

BELA LUGOSI

Actor Bela Lugosi, who portrayed the infamous Count Dracula in feature films, was actually born in Transylvania and took his last name from his hometown, Lugos. He spent his early years as an actor in Sibiu, a quiet medieval town tucked in the Carpathian Mountains, not far from the legendary Castle Dracula in the Brogo Pass. It is very probable that Bela himself had a "blood" relation to his most famous role.

Boris Karloff

Actor Boris Karloff, best known for his roles in *The Mummy* and *Frankenstein*, is related to Anna, governess to the king of Siam, whose story was first popularized by her autobiography and then was made into the film *The King and I*.

BORIS KARLOFF

The roots of the relationship between two such diverse personalities as Karloff and Anna lies in the civil service during the British rule in India. Karloff came from a family of foreign service officers, and it was only natural for his aunt Anna to go to India as the wife of a young officer. When Anna's husband was killed on a tiger hunt, she was stranded alone in India with two young children. In search of a job, she ran into the Siamese consul, who was under orders from the king to find a female teacher for the royal children. The king was convinced that he must bring his feudal country into the nineteenth century with the education of the royal children.

From contemporary accounts, Anna appears to have been very similar to the strong-willed woman portrayed by Deborah Kerr in the movie *The King and I*. When Anna finally left Siam, the king said to Anna: "I am often angry at you and lose my temper, though I have a large respect for you. But nevertheless, you ought to know you are a difficult woman, and more difficult than generally."

Immediately upon leaving Siam, Anna began writing, and her first article describing her adventures in Siam appeared in 1869. Instantly she was a sensation. Everyone wanted her to lecture, and she became the darling of New York literary society, rubbing shoulders with James Russell Lowell, Oliver Wendell Holmes, William Cullen Bryant, Henry Wadsworth Longfellow, and Ralph Waldo Emerson.

In 1897, thirty years after she left Siam, Anna saw her most distinguished pupil, the crown prince, in London. He had been king for twenty-nine years, the old king having died within a year of Anna's departure. Anna's teachings had had a profound effect on the young prince. In conformance with Anna's teaching, he had abolished slavery, started schools, imported missionaries, and substituted educated officials for the old feudal administrators. His country was on the road to modernization, and in his own lifetime the Siamese had already proclaimed him their greatest king. Anna, through her influence over the young prince, had changed a whole country!

Lon Chaney

Actor Lon Chaney, the man of a thousand faces on the silent screen and the first *Phantom of the Opera*, grew up using his hands, face, and body to communicate without sound: both of his parents, Frank Chaney and Emma Kennedy, were deaf.

Frank Chaney was a barber, and one of his earliest customers in Cheyenne, Wyoming, was General George Armstrong Custer. Frank Chaney visited the battlefield the day after the massacre at Little Bighorn and was relieved to discover that while the Indians had scalped the other 208 soldiers, they had not touched Custer's hair.

Jonathan R. Kennedy, Lon Chaney's grandfather, had gone to Kansas in the early days and had fought with John Brown. In 1873 he moved to Denver, where, because of his three deaf children, Martha, Emma, and Oliver, he actively petitioned the legislature for the creation of a school for the deaf in Colorado. In 1874 the legislature voted to establish the school in Colorado Springs and chose Kennedy as the first superintendent. This school evolved into what is today the Deaf and Blind Institute of Colorado.

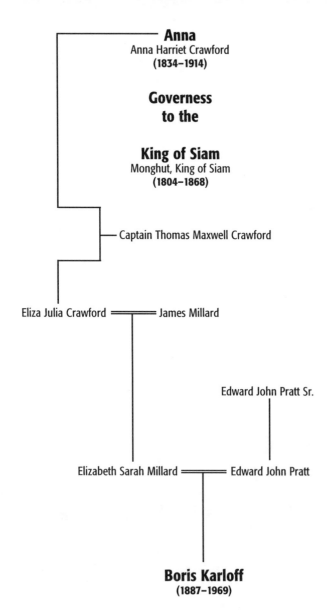

Anna
Anna Harriet Crawford
(1834–1914)

**Governess
to the**

King of Siam
Monghut, King of Siam
(1804–1868)

Captain Thomas Maxwell Crawford

Eliza Julia Crawford ══════ James Millard

Edward John Pratt Sr.

Elizabeth Sarah Millard ══════ Edward John Pratt

Boris Karloff
(1887–1969)

Five

FOUNDERS

The English colonies in America, which eventually became the United States, didn't just appear on their own. It took men of vision, men looking for freedom, or maybe just men looking to make a buck, but whatever their motivation, it was their drive and leadership which gave this country its start.

Michael Douglas	≋	Peter Stuyvesant (New York)
Charles Coburn	≋	Roger Williams (Rhode Island)
Jane Wyatt	≋	William Patterson (New Jersey)
Gloria Vanderbilt	≋	Roger Williams (Rhode Island)

Michael Douglas

Film star Michael Douglas, while he doesn't do a lot of his own genealogical research, has an uncle in Bermuda who does, and he turned his papers over to the author. Michael Douglas's uncle used to be the attorney general of the island and was knighted by the queen. When the author delved into the Dill family vaults, he turned up Peter Stuyvesant, the one-legged Dutch governor of New York, as a relative.

MICHAEL DOUGLAS

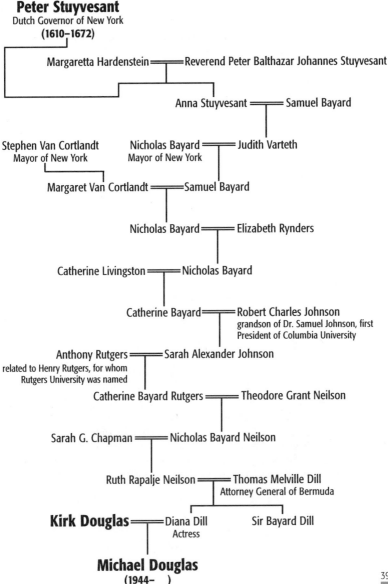

Peter Stuyvesant
Dutch Governor of New York
(1610–1672)

Margaretta Hardenstein ══════ Reverend Peter Balthazar Johannes Stuyvesant

Anna Stuyvesant ═════ Samuel Bayard

Stephen Van Cortlandt
Mayor of New York

Nicholas Bayard ═════ Judith Varteth
Mayor of New York

Margaret Van Cortlandt ═════ Samuel Bayard

Nicholas Bayard ═════ Elizabeth Rynders

Catherine Livingston ═════ Nicholas Bayard

Catherine Bayard ═════ Robert Charles Johnson
grandson of Dr. Samuel Johnson, first
President of Columbia University

Anthony Rutgers ═════ Sarah Alexander Johnson
related to Henry Rutgers, for whom
Rutgers University was named

Catherine Bayard Rutgers ═════ Theodore Grant Neilson

Sarah G. Chapman ═════ Nicholas Bayard Neilson

Ruth Rapalje Neilson ═════ Thomas Melville Dill
Attorney General of Bermuda

Kirk Douglas ═════ Diana Dill   Sir Bayard Dill
Actress

Michael Douglas
(1944–   )

39

PETER STUYVESANT

Peter Stuyvesant's first accomplishment upon arriving in New Amsterdam was the erection of a wall across Manhattan, later known as "Wall Street," to protect the struggling colony from the Indians. Later his relation Michael Douglas would make the film *Wall Street*.

For years Peter Stuyvesant tried to improve the fort, or "battery," at the end of the island, but the good citizens of New Amsterdam did not want to pay the taxes necessary for the defense of the city. As a result, the fort became a public joke. In good times or bad, there stood the fort, like a comic albatross, bearing down upon the town the cost of its repairs, which never lasted, and with its dismal appearance, an affront to the town's dignity.

KIRK DOUGLAS

Ultimately, Charles II, the recently restored king of England, made a present to his brother, the duke of York, of New Amsterdam, neglecting to mention the fact that the city was actually the colony of another country. The duke,

THOMAS MELVILLE DILL

who was also the Lord High Admiral of England, thanked his brother for the gift and then assembled a fleet of four warships. On August 26, 1664, the English fleet sailed past Governor's Island and stationed itself off the Battery, effectively blockading the city. A letter demanding immediate surrender undermined any possibility that Stuyvesant would get any help from his citizens, because it promised the Dutch burgers that they could keep their property if the city surrendered, but their lands would be forfeit if they resisted. With great fanfare, the English entered the city and renamed it after the duke of York.

Cecil B. De Mille

Film director Cecil B. De Mille is descended from Anthony De Mille, who came from Holland in the ship *Gilded Beaver*, which Cecil later used as the name of the colonial inn in his film *Unconquered*. Anthony's son Peter became the mayor of New Amsterdam.

Family history can often come to bear on film projects. The Dutch, the original settlers of New Amsterdam before it became New York, counted among those early settlers Anthony De Mille and Jelles Douwese Fonda. When descendants Cecil B. De Mille and Henry Fonda decided to make *Drums Along the Mohawk*, they were intrigued by the fact that they were reliving the adventures of their own Dutch ancestors.

John Derek

Producer John Derek, the mentor of his wife, Bo Derek, had as an immigrant ancestor Robert Clements. Clements was born in England in 1595 and was a founder of the town of Haverhill, Massachusetts.

Charles Coburn

CHARLES COBURN

Character actor Charles Coburn is directly descended from Roger Williams, the founder of Rhode Island and the first colonial governor to allow religious freedom, a basic freedom later incorporated into the U.S. Constitution. When Williams landed in the Massachusetts Bay Colony, he insisted on the separation of church and state, refusing to allow the magistrate to punish anyone for religious offenses such as blasphemy or heresy. Because of his important position as the minister at Salem, he was viewed as a threat to the entire colony. The colony leaders were determined to deport him to England, where he could do no harm, but he fled in the middle of a blizzard to Narragansett, where he made friends with the Indians, helped them in a dispute, and received land in return for his help. He named this new land Providence. The watchword of the new colony was religious freedom, and soon settlers were swarming there to escape the inflexible religious rule of John Winthrop in Massachusetts.

Howard Hawks

Director Howard Hawks was the brother of director Kenneth Hawks and producer William Hawks. Their immigrant ancestor was John Hawks of

Hadley, Massachusetts, and Windsor, Connecticut, freeman of the General Court of Massachusetts Bay Colony in 1634.

Raymond Massey

Actor Raymond Massey's immigrant ancestor was Geoffrey Massey Jr., who sailed in 1629 from Bristol, England, on the ship *Lyon*, part of the great fleet that accompanied Governor John Winthrop, the man who helped settle Salem, Massachusetts.

Treat Williams

Film star Treat Williams is related to Robert Treat Paine, a signer of the Declaration of Independence, and to Governor Robert Treat of Connecticut. Like brave men generally, Governor Treat appears to have been exceedingly timid and backward in the

TREAT WILLIAMS

presence of the fair sex. That is to say, he was extremely slow in getting to the point—a proposal of marriage. While danc-

ROBERT TREAT PAINE

ing his future wife, Jane Tapp, on his knee—as was permissible by their disparity of age and long intimacy—the damsel brought her lover to a prompt decision by the suggestive expostulation, "Robert, be still that I had rather be *Treat*ed than trotted."

Jane Wyatt

Actress Jane Wyatt is descended from Anne Hutchinson, the first woman radical advocate in America. Anne Hutchinson had emigrated to America in 1634 to follow her minister, the Reverend John Cotton, to Massachusetts. She was soon at loggerheads with Governor John Winthrop, and she was ultimately excommunicated from the church.

JANE WYATT

The basis of their dispute was religious freedom. Anne Hutchinson tried to conduct services in her own home, and when she couldn't, she took her family and tried to start a new colony in the area now known as Rhode Island. However, Winthrop was after her even there, and when her son went back to Boston, Winthrop had him arrested, fined, and thrown into prison. Afraid for herself and her family, she tried to get further away and moved down the coast to New York. There, she and her family were massacred. Winthrop claimed that she was killed by Indians, but the true story is that men from Massachusetts hired the Indians to make sure that Anne was silenced forever. Nine members of her family were murdered with her, and one daughter was carried into captivity with the Indians. When the daughter was released she had forgotten how to speak English.

Patrick Swayze

The star of *Dirty Dancing* and the TV miniseries *North and South* is a descendant of the pioneer Reverend Samuel Swayze. In 1772, just prior to the American Revolution, he led his congregation from Perth Amboy, New Jersey, to Kingston, just outside of Natchez, Mississippi, where they settled on a land grant that was sold to them by a Captain Amos Ogden, who had received the land for his service in the French and Indian War.

Six

NATIVE AMERICANS

Not all Native Americans fit the stereotype (i.e., live on reservations and run casinos). Most often, you wouldn't even know they were natives. After all, is Dolly Parton your idea of what Pocahontas looked like? Here's a list of Native Americans, many of whom it probably never even occurred to you were Indians.

Pocahontas
Wayne Newton
Jack Holt and Tim Holt
Edith Bolling Wilson (Mrs. Woodrow Wilson)
Chief Justice John Marshall

Pocahontas

POCAHONTAS

Probably one of the single most famous Indians in history is Pocahontas. Among her more distinguished descendants are singer Wayne Newton, Mrs. Woodrow Wilson, actors Jack Holt and Tim Holt, and Chief Justice John Marshall.

Pocahontas became famous in England after Captain John Smith published an account of how she had saved his life. Smith had established tobac-

WOODROW WILSON

EDITH BOLLING WILSON

co as a cash crop to put the colony on a sound fiscal footing, and he decided that Pocahontas was just the person to get publicity for their product. He sent her to England—where she arrived just after the death of Shakespeare—with a mission to show everyone how "cool" it was to smoke. Pocahontas was presented to the king and queen, who were infatuated with the Indian princess at once. The king wanted to know if her son would become king of America.

WAYNE NEWTON

Pocahontas became the toast of London. One smart bar, looking to cash in on her popularity and drum up some business, changed its name to La Belle Savage. Her publicity mission must have been successful, judging by the millions smoking today.

Cherokees
Kim Basinger
Dolly Parton (one-eighth)
Anita Bryant
Johnny Cash (one-quarter)
Richard Chamberlain
Cher
Johnny Depp
Sandy Duncan
James Garner
Jimi Hendrix
Waylon Jennings
Eartha Kitt
Moms Mabley
Sally Field
Lou Diamond Phillips

KIM BASINGER

WAYLON JENNINGS

Jon Peters (one-half)
John Phillips (one-half)
Robert Rauschenberg (one-quarter)
Oral Roberts
Dennis Weaver
Burt Reynolds
Kevin Costner
Chuck Norris
Linda Darnell
Will Rogers

Choctaws

KEVIN COSTNER

Farrah Fawcett
Roy Rogers

Creeks

Pearl Bailey

Comanches

Waylon Jennings
Tommy Lee Jones

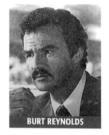

BURT REYNOLDS

Blackfeet

Lena Horne
Robert Mitchum
John Mitchum
James Mitchum
Chris Mitchum
Johnnie Ray

Shawnees

Tommy Tune

ROBERT MITCHUM

Seven

THE MAYFLOWER

The *Mayflower* brought the first group of settlers to New England, common folk who created the legend of America as the land of opportunity. The first winter killed most of them, leaving fifty-four survivors, twenty-one of them under the age of 16. After the starvation of the first winter, the Pilgrims were thankful to be alive, and when the first harvest came in a bumper crop, Governor William Bradford called for a feast: the first Thanksgiving. The following celebrities all had ancestors who came over on the *Mayflower*.

Hugh Hefner
Vincent Price
Stephen King
Marilyn Monroe
Orson Welles
Raquel Welch
Bing Crosby
Humphrey Bogart
Johnny Carson

Laura Ingalls
Jane Wyatt
Alan Shepard
Edie Adams
Richard Dix
Robert Altman
Mayflower Madam
(Sydney Biddle Barrows)

Mayflower Madam (Sydney Biddle Barrows)

Sydney Biddle Barrows, who gained notoriety for the string of exclusive call girls she ran in New York, claims descent from *Mayflower* passenger Elder William Brewster, the minister at Plymouth. He might have had a sermon or two to preach about this descendant of his!

Hugh Hefner

HUGH HEFNER

Publisher Hugh Hefner, who helped with his creation of *Playboy* to free this country from the Puritan code that gripped its sex life for four centuries, is the direct descendant of William Bradford, who became the first governor of the Pilgrims from the *Mayflower*, and who founded the Plymouth Colony. Bradford later wrote his *History of Plymouth Plantation*, the complete story of the Pilgrims' flight to Holland and their subsequent journey to the New World. Hef is so proud of this *Mayflower* ancestry that he named his son Cooper Bradford Hefner.

Humphrey Bogart and Stephen King

HUMPHREY BOGART

Actor Humphrey Bogart and horror writer Stephen King's *Mayflower* ancestor, John Howland, almost didn't make it to America. There were many savage storms, and during one of them Howland was swept overboard. He grabbed one of the topsail halyards as he went over and grimly hung on,

STEPHEN KING

dragged behind the ship, yelling for help when he was able to surface. Finally, several men began hauling in the rope. He had swallowed a lot of green water, but he survived and lived to the ripe old age of 80.

Laura Ingalls

Author Laura Ingalls Wilder was the creator of the *Little House on the Prairie* books, which were later made famous by Michael Landon's TV

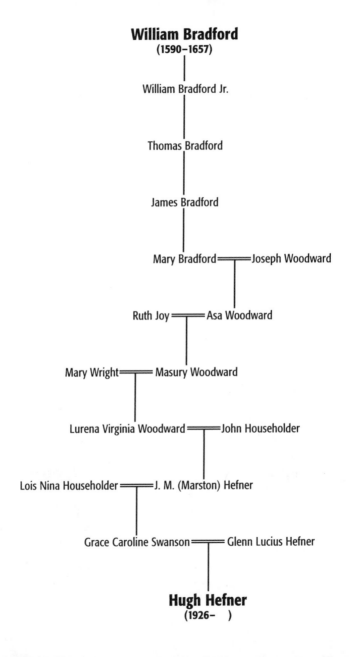

series. Although she went west in a covered wagon, Laura Ingalls lived long and came back east on a jet airplane. Her ancestor who came over on the *Mayflower*, Stephen Hopkins, opened up the first bar in America. In 1637 he was fined for "suffering servants and others to sit drinking in his house upon the Lord's Day, before the meeting ended." In other words, they should have been in church, rather than at his bar.

Marilyn Monroe

It is interesting to speculate how the movie version of Longfellow's poem "The Courtship of Myles Standish" would have played out with Marilyn Monroe in the role of her ancestor Priscilla Mullins.

The story is essentially a Pilgrim love triangle. Myles Standish does not realize his friend John Alden is in love with Priscilla when he asks him to speak on his behalf. John sings the praises of Myles Standish, only to have Priscilla demand, "Why don't you speak for yourself, John?"

MARILYN MONROE

While Marilyn Monroe never knew the father through whom she descended from John Alden and Priscilla Mullins, she was obsessed with him. Marilyn transferred her father-worship to her husbands. Marilyn always called her first husband, Jim Doughtery, "Daddy." In his letters to Marilyn, her husband Joe DiMaggio signed himself "Pa." During her marriage to Arthur Miller, she called him "Poppy" or "Pa." Once, at a New York party, Marilyn took part in a game in which she had to say what she wanted most in the world. Her reply was that she would "like to put on her black wig, pick up her father in a bar, and have him make love to her."

Vincent Price

Vincent Price claims descent from Peregrine White, the first *Mayflower* child, born in New England on board the ship while it lay at anchor in Plymouth Bay in 1620. He was also the last of the ship's passengers to die, living to see the Plymouth Colony absorbed by Massachusetts in 1691, and was still alive to usher in the new century in 1700.

VINCENT PRICE

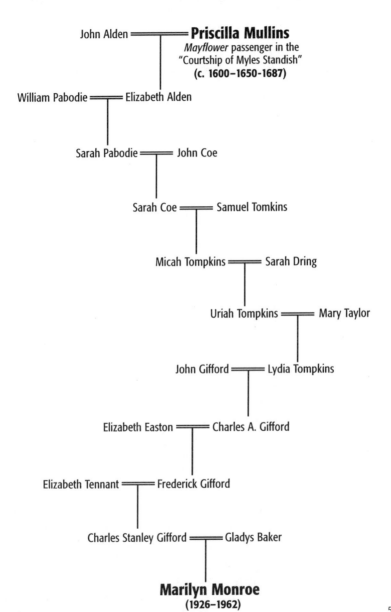

John Alden ══════ **Priscilla Mullins**
Mayflower passenger in the
"Courtship of Myles Standish"
(c. 1600–1650–1687)

William Pabodie ══════ Elizabeth Alden

Sarah Pabodie ══════ John Coe

Sarah Coe ══════ Samuel Tomkins

Micah Tompkins ══════ Sarah Dring

Uriah Tompkins ══════ Mary Taylor

John Gifford ══════ Lydia Tompkins

Elizabeth Easton ══════ Charles A. Gifford

Elizabeth Tennant ══════ Frederick Gifford

Charles Stanley Gifford ══════ Gladys Baker

Marilyn Monroe
(1926–1962)

Eight

ROYALS

◎◎

Brooke Shields	≋	Lucrezia Borgia
Rene Auberjonois	≋	Napoleon
Catherine Oxenberg	≋	Catherine the Great
Oliver Reed	≋	Peter the Great
Jane Fonda	≋	Jane Seymour
Basil Rathbone	≋	Henry IV
Richard Nixon	≋	Edward III
Rachel Ward	≋	Henry VIII
Angela Lansbury	≋	Robert the Bruce
Gloria Grahame	≋	Edward III
Karl Marx	≋	Robert the Bruce
Joanne Woodward	≋	Charlemagne
Elizabeth Lindsey	≋	King Kamehameha of Hawaii
Audrey Hepburn	≋	Elizabeth II
Ernest Borgnine	≋	Count Boselli, Adviser to King Victor Emmanuel
Yul Brynner	≋	Genghis Khan
John D. Rockefeller	≋	Elizabeth I
Jack London	≋	Edward I
Burt Lancaster	≋	English House of Lancaster
Michael Wilding	≋	John of Gaunt
Shelley Winters	≋	Katie Schratt, Mistress of Emperor Franz Joseph of Austria-Hungary
Jack Lemmon	≋	Earl of Gainsborough
Christopher Lee	≋	Lucrezia Borgia
Princess Diana	≋	Nathan Hale
Patrick Macnee	≋	Robin Hood
Elizabeth II	≋	Meriwether Lewis

Brooke Shields

BROOKE SHIELDS

The story of actress Brooke Shields's remarkable ancestry actually begins with Brooke's grandfather, Francis Xavier Shields, a drop-dead handsome tennis star and glittering bon vivant. Frank Shields was a torch of insatiable pleasures running in the fast tracks from Newport to Hollywood. All doors were open to him, from the bedrooms of the most sought-after beauties to the private offices of the richest tycoons. From Greta Garbo and Norma Shearer to Marilyn Monroe, the starlets fell for him. He married Italian princess Marina Torlonia, who descended from Lucrezia Borgia, the sister of Cesare Borgia, whose evil brilliance and determination was already a legend in his own time when he was idealized by Machiavelli in his book *The Prince*.

In her very own *Brooke Book*, published in 1978, Brooke Shields states that she once tested for the role of Lucrezia Borgia with director Danelle Sentore. However, the career of Lucrezia Borgia is in striking contrast to Brooke's own life and accomplishments. The saintly Shields appears to have little in common with her Borgia ancestors.

LUCREZIA BORGIA

Lucrezia's father the pope had already lain with her, as had her brother Juan. Having engaged in incest and debauchery, it was only left for the happy Borgia family to engage in the most heinous crime of all. Cesare, the older brother, was so infatuated with his sister that when he learned of his brother Juan's relationship with her, he killed him. Juan's body, full of daggers, was later found floating in the Tiber. With his brother out of the way, Cesare was finally able to debauch his sister.

Karl Marx

Karl Marx, the man who created the idea of Communism with his book *Das Kapital*, was himself obsessed with the aristocracy. Far from wanting to be a comrade, he was much more interested in obtaining a noble title

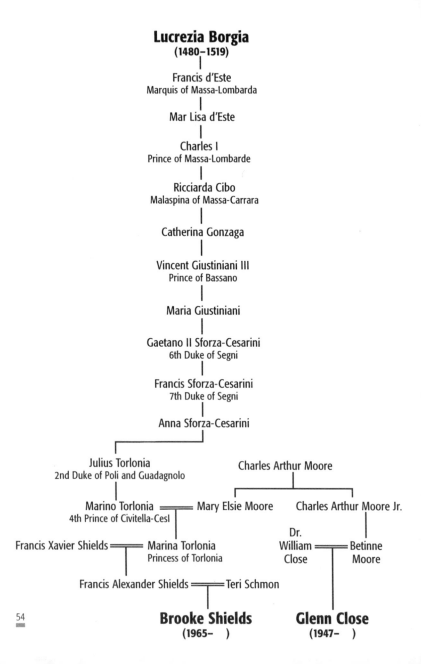

Lucrezia Borgia
(1480–1519)

Francis d'Este
Marquis of Massa-Lombarda

Mar Lisa d'Este

Charles I
Prince of Massa-Lombarde

Ricciarda Cibo
Malaspina of Massa-Carrara

Catherina Gonzaga

Vincent Giustiniani III
Prince of Bassano

Maria Giustiniani

Gaetano II Sforza-Cesarini
6th Duke of Segni

Francis Sforza-Cesarini
7th Duke of Segni

Anna Sforza-Cesarini

Julius Torlonia
2nd Duke of Poli and Guadagnolo

Charles Arthur Moore

Marino Torlonia ═══ Mary Elsie Moore
4th Prince of Civitella-Cesl

Charles Arthur Moore Jr.

Francis Xavier Shields ═══ Marina Torlonia
Princess of Torlonia

Dr.
William ═══ Betinne
Close   Moore

Francis Alexander Shields ═══ Teri Schmon

Brooke Shields
(1965–   )

Glenn Close
(1947–   )

for himself. While he couldn't change his parents, he did the next best thing and married into royalty. His wife, Jenny von Westphalen, was a direct descendant of Robert the Bruce, probably the most famous of the Scottish kings, who reestablished the independence of Scotland.

Robert the Bruce had been at war with the English, led by King Edward I, and had been soundly defeated, requiring him to go into hiding for fear of losing his life. He decided he would have a better claim to the throne if he had himself crowned king of Scotland. The woman who crowned him, the countess of Buchan, had been captured by the English and suspended in a metal cage for four years from the wall of Berwick Castle…an ordeal she survived!

Rachel Ward

Actress Rachel Ward is the eldest daughter of Peter, the earl of Dudley, whose ancestral seat is Cornwall Manor near Oxford, England, and through him she is related to Henry VIII. Through her mother, Claire Leonora Baring, she has American ancestry, being a descendant of William Bingham, a senator. Bingham was very active in land speculation after the Revolution, and one monument to his land deals is the town of Binghamton, New York.

Rene Auberjonois

RENE AUBERJONOIS

Rene Auberjonois, who played Father Mulcahy in the feature film *M*A*S*H* and portrays Security Chief Odo on the television series *Deep Space Nine*, is related to Napoleon Bonaparte, the self-proclaimed emperor of France. Napoleon bit off more than he could chew when he invaded Russia and most of his army was destroyed. After his defeat, afraid that his enemies would take control of the government, Napoleon rushed back to France, leaving his army behind. Outdistancing his bodyguard and alone in his sleigh, he reached the River Neman and asked the ferryman if he had seen any deserters come that way. "No, sir," was the reply. "You are the first."

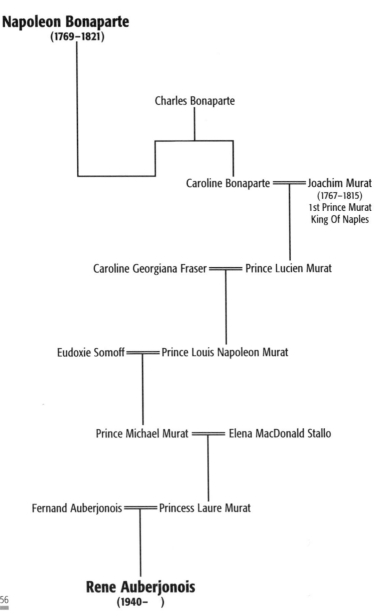

Napoleon Bonaparte
(1769–1821)

Charles Bonaparte

Caroline Bonaparte ══ Joachim Murat
(1767–1815)
1st Prince Murat
King Of Naples

Caroline Georgiana Fraser ══ Prince Lucien Murat

Eudoxie Somoff ══ Prince Louis Napoleon Murat

Prince Michael Murat ══ Elena MacDonald Stallo

Fernand Auberjonois ══ Princess Laure Murat

Rene Auberjonois
(1940–)

Gloria Grahame

GLORIA GRAHAME

Oscar-winning actress Gloria Grahame (*It's A Wonderful Life, Oklahoma!*) is not only a direct descendant of Edward III, but she has some other interesting twigs on her family tree.

Her grandfather, Reginald Francis Hallward, was a great friend of Oscar Wilde. As a portrait painter, Hallward had suggested to Wilde that it would be clever if the model stayed young but the portrait became old. Oscar immediately went home and wrote *The Picture of Dorian Gray*, and just so there would be no mistake about who gave him the idea, the name of the painter in the story became Basil Hallward. This would have been flattering, except for the fact that the painter in the story leads Dorian into a life of sexual depravity and perversion, and is murdered by him in the end.

Joanne Woodward

JOANNE WOODWARD

Joanne Gignilliat Woodward, actress and wife of Paul Newman, has a remarkable ancestry. It is very unusual for an immigrant to America to have a royal descent from the Continental royal houses. After all, as one noble was quick to exclaim, "Dukes don't emigrate." On the Continent each descendant of the nobility carries a title, which carries with it perks that few want to give up. However, an exception was Jean-François Gignilliat, an early Swiss emigrant to South Carolina. His 1685 grant from the Lords Proprietors of Carolina mentioned his "Testimony of his Honorable Extraction." He was descended from the kings of France, reaching all the way back to Charlemagne himself.

Joanne is also a descendant of Charlemagne, to whose wife can be credited the invention of white wine. Charlemagne was quite a slob when he was eating, and would always get red wine all over his beard. His wife, totally fed up with his manners, ordered that the vineyards produce a white grape so that he would not look such a mess!

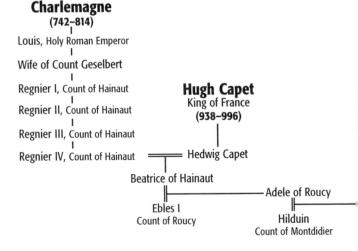

Charlemagne
(742–814)

Louis, Holy Roman Emperor

Wife of Count Geselbert

Regnier I, Count of Hainaut

Regnier II, Count of Hainaut

Regnier III, Count of Hainaut

Regnier IV, Count of Hainaut ===== Hedwig Capet

Hugh Capet
King of France
(938–996)

Beatrice of Hainaut

Ebles I
Count of Roucy

Adele of Roucy

Hilduin
Count of Montdidier

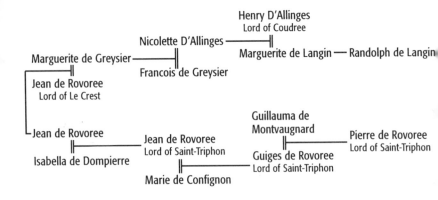

Henry D'Allinges
Lord of Coudree

Nicolette D'Allinges ———

Marguerite de Langin — Randolph de Langin

Marguerite de Greysier ———

Francois de Greysier

Jean de Rovoree
Lord of Le Crest

Jean de Rovoree

Isabella de Dompierre

Jean de Rovoree
Lord of Saint-Triphon

Marie de Confignon

Guillauma de
Montvaugnard

Guiges de Rovoree
Lord of Saint-Triphon

Pierre de Rovoree
Lord of Saint-Triphon

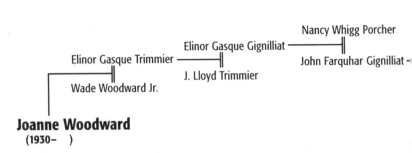

Nancy Whigg Porcher

Elinor Gasque Gignilliat ———

John Farquhar Gignilliat

Elinor Gasque Trimmier ———

J. Lloyd Trimmier

Wade Woodward Jr.

Joanne Woodward
(1930–)

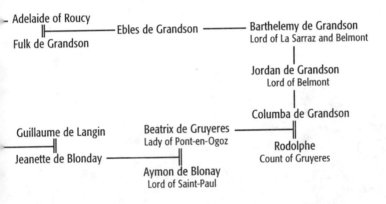

Adelaide of Roucy
Fulk de Grandson
— Ebles de Grandson — Barthelemy de Grandson
Lord of La Sarraz and Belmont

Jordan de Grandson
Lord of Belmont

Columba de Grandson

Guillaume de Langin
Jeanette de Blonday
Beatrix de Gruyeres
Lady of Pont-en-Ogoz
Rodolphe
Count of Gruyeres

Aymon de Blonay
Lord of Saint-Paul

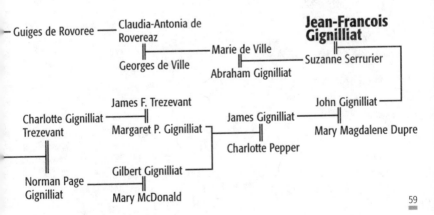

Guiges de Rovoree
Claudia-Antonia de Rovereaz
Georges de Ville
Jean-Francois Gignilliat

Marie de Ville
Abraham Gignilliat
Suzanne Serrurier

James F. Trezevant
Charlotte Gignilliat Trezevant
Margaret P. Gignilliat
James Gignilliat
Charlotte Pepper
John Gignilliat
Mary Magdalene Dupre

Norman Page Gignilliat
Gilbert Gignilliat
Mary McDonald

Audrey Hepburn

William Wyler, when he was casting *Roman Holiday* with Gregory Peck, said, "I wanted a girl without an American accent to play the princess, someone you could believe was brought up a princess." Audrey Hepburn fit that bill, and this was the film that launched her career. Her mother was the Baroness Ella Van Heemstra and was descended from a long line of aristocrats connected directly to the royal court of Holland. Their ancestral residence was the Castle of Doorn, which is now open to the public as a stately home and museum. Hepburn's grandfather, Baron Aernoud Van Heemstra, was governor of Dutch Guiana (Surinam).

AUDREY HEPBURN

Audrey Hepburn also had royal ties through her relation to Anne Boleyn, wife of Henry VIII and mother of Elizabeth I, the Virgin Queen of England. Therefore, she was a cousin to Elizabeth II.

John D. Rockefeller

JOHN D. ROCKEFELLER

Industrialist John D. Rockfeller was a cousin to Elizabeth I, queen of England. Elizabeth encouraged Sir Francis Drake and his cohorts to raid Spanish gold ships, and although she disavowed this in public, in private she shared the loot. On one occasion, the earl of Oxford, standing before the queen, broke wind. He was so mortified that he left the country for ten years. On his return to England and the court, Queen Elizabeth looked right at him and said, "Are you going to fart again?"

Jack London

Writer Jack London, through his mother, Flora Wellman, was related to film director William Wellman. He was also a direct descendant of King Edward I of England, through his sixth great-grandmother, Jane Deighton.

Basil Rathbone

Actor Basil Rathbone was the best swordsman in Hollywood, a skill he picked up as an officer in the British army during World War I, where he was decorated in the field. Although his villainous roles called for him to lose most fights, he always took comfort in the knowledge that he could have easily defeated any opponent in a real duel. Even though he was born in South Africa, he came from an English gentry family. His first cousin, Eleanor Rathbone, was the first woman ever elected to the British Parliament, and his uncle, Herbert Rathbone, was Lord Mayor of Liverpool.

BASIL RATHBONE

Basil Rathbone's mother was a descendant of Henry IV. Henry was consumed with a desire to lead a crusade to the Holy Land, and was therefore quite pleased when a soothsayer told him he would die in Jerusalem. However, after a heart attack he was brought to rest in a room called the Jerusalem Chamber! He was so upset when he realized his true fate that he died from aggravation.

Richard M. Nixon

Richard M. Nixon, former president of the United States, was a descendant of King Edward III of England. In Paris for the funeral of French president Georges Pompidou in 1974, Nixon flubbed, stating, "This is a great day for France."

Burt Lancaster

Actor Burt Lancaster claims that his ancestry can be traced to England's royal house of Lancaster. The house of Lancaster was in perpetual conflict with the house of York, culminating in a bloody civil war in the 1400s, called the War of the Roses, that raged between these two royal houses for control of the throne of England.

Oliver Reed

Actor Oliver Reed claims to be the illegitimate great-great-grandson of Czar Peter the Great of Russia, as the result of Peter's dalliance in England during his grand tour. This is entirely possible, considering Peter's reputation for debauchery.

Everywhere that Peter stayed in England, he worked hard and played hard. He destroyed numerous houses at which he stayed. One landlord reported that every single painting, window, and piece of furniture in the house had been completely smashed. His landlords could not even begin to dream how so much destruction could be wreaked on their property, but they ceased to complain when the bills were paid.

Catherine Oxenberg

CATHERINE OXENBERG

Actress Catherine Oxenberg, star of TV's *Dynasty*, is a direct descendant of Catherine the Great, the most famous woman ruler of Russia, who married Czar Peter III at the age of 16. It didn't take her long to discover that her new husband was an idiot, and she had him murdered within six months. However, not being Russian, she was not secure on the throne, and at one point her field artillery had to pound some 200,000 peasants into submission. When the middle class revolted, she was obliged to slaughter them as well. However, she recognized that Russia was primitive and backward by European standards, and she did all that she could to ensure that Russia became enlightened under her rule, hence the suffix "the Great" added to her name.

Peter Ustinov

PETER USTINOV

Actor Peter Ustinov's ancestor Adrian Mihalovitch Ustinov made a fortune in the salt business in Siberia, allowing him to rise into the nobility, and he then proudly put a salt press on his coat of arms. His son, Mihail Andrianovitch Ustinoff, took advantage of a decree in which Catherine the Great promised a tract of land for every sheep raised. He soon had so many sheep that he received a huge estate, and when he died the estate had 6,000 serfs.

Anthony Quinn

Actor Anthony Quinn's father, Frank Quinn, was an Irish adventurer who had fought with Pancho Villa during the latter's escapades in Mexico. Through his mother, Manuela Oaxaca, he can claim descent from the ancient Aztec royalty that ruled in Mexico prior to the incursion of the Spanish conquistador Cortez.

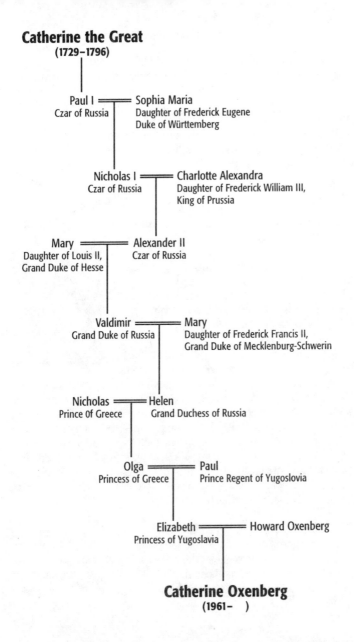

Catherine the Great
(1729–1796)

Paul I === Sophia Maria
Czar of Russia — Daughter of Frederick Eugene
Duke of Württemberg

Nicholas I === Charlotte Alexandra
Czar of Russia — Daughter of Frederick William III,
King of Prussia

Mary === Alexander II
Daughter of Louis II, — Czar of Russia
Grand Duke of Hesse

Valdimir === Mary
Grand Duke of Russia — Daughter of Frederick Francis II,
Grand Duke of Mecklenburg-Schwerin

Nicholas === Helen
Prince Of Greece — Grand Duchess of Russia

Olga === Paul
Princess of Greece — Prince Regent of Yugoslovia

Elizabeth === Howard Oxenberg
Princess of Yugoslavia

Catherine Oxenberg
(1961–)

The most notable attribute of the Aztecs was their ritual sacrifice of human beings. They sacrificed men, women, and children, and sometimes the carnage was extensive. The children they needed were often taken from their mothers at an early age and prepared in a sort of "priests' kindergarten" for the ritual slaughter. Aside from the routine daily sacrifices, a special event like the dedication of a new temple called for a really large ceremony, in one case 20,000 captives being sacrificed to the newly completed temple of Huitzilopochtli.

Yul Brynner

Actor Yul Brynner, whose credits include his epic *Taras Bulba*, was actually descended from the leader of the Mongolian hordes he portrayed. In

the 1860s, Yul's Swiss grandfather Jules Brynner took his export business to Vladivostok, where he married Natalia Kurkutova, the daughter of a Mongolian prince, the sister of the chief justice of Vladivostok, and a descendant of Genghis Khan. His name Jules was changed to Yul in Russian, and his grandson was named after him.

YUL BRYNNER

Genghis Khan, named Temuchin at birth, created his name by combining Genghis, which meant "perfect warrior," with Khan, meaning "king." Originally the chief of a small tribe, by conquest he became the leader of all Mongols, and then of all China. The self-styled "Emperor of All Men," he was one of the most bloodthirsty leaders in history. In one week he ordered 1.6 million people tortured and killed. Arms and legs were hacked off, and then the screaming trunks were flung into the road to roll helplessly away and die in agony. Children, a dozen or more at a time, were skewered like shish kebab on lances, and then burnt alive in great wailing heaps while their mothers, hideously mutilated, were forced to watch.

Christopher Lee

Actor Christopher Carandini Lee is a hereditary count of the Holy Roman Empire, a position that gives him the privilege of a private audience with the pope. A cousin of his mother was Count Niccolo Carandini, Italy's first post-war ambassador to Britain, who helped him get his first acting role.

Lee's mother, Contessa Estele Marie Carandini, was a descendant of one of Italy's oldest families. The Carandinis featured prominently in the affairs of the Holy Roman Empire, holding the contracts for supplying the chariots to the Roman army. His relationship to Lucrezia Borgia might well explain his success in horror films!

Ernest Borgnine

Oscar-winning star Ernest Borgnine is an Italian count whose grandfather Count Boselli was an adviser to King Victor Emmanuel.

Shelley Winters

Oscar-winning actress Shelley Winters was once warned about a certain Italian producer by her publicist. He said, "He's a terrible wolf. He'll tear the clothes off your back." Shelley snapped back, "So I'll wear an old dress."

SHELLEY WINTERS

Shelley Winter's great-aunt was actress Katie Schratt, who became the mistress of Emperor Franz Joseph of Austria-Hungary. For twenty-seven years they were seen constantly together. In the court theater she was a great comedienne, but it was her emotional support to the emperor that was her real value to the empire. She was always bubbly, and could keep him in good spirits if not good health, baking him little cakes in the form of handkerchiefs when he had a cold. She fed him not only goulash but also the backstage gossip that he relished.

Jack Lemmon

Jack Lemmon is descended from the ancient Noel family, whose name has been continued in the family, as his son, actor Chris Lemmon, named Jack's first grandchild Sydney Noel Lemmon. Jack's ancestor Baptist Noel was an early colonist in Virginia, arriving from England about the year 1700. The Noel family appears to have originally taken its name from Noailles, Normandy, France, where they were dukes. One branch of the family came to England with William the Conqueror, as recorded in the Domesday Book, where the head of the family was granted the titles of the Baron Noel and earl of Gainsborough.

William Bendix

Actor William Bendix is a descendant of composer Felix Mendelssohn, and thus he is also descended from the remarkable Saul Wahl-Katzenellenbogen, Saul Wahl to his friends, who was unanimously elected king of Poland. Other notable descendants of this family include Karl Marx, the cosmetics manufacturer Helena Rubinstein, and Pulitzer Prize-winning author David Halberstam.

How did Saul Wahl come to be so trusted by the nobles of Poland? Prince Radziwill of Poland was traveling abroad and ran out of money in Italy. Penniless, he was given a substantial loan by Saul's father, a rabbi. When Prince Radziwill returned home, he granted Saul many favors. For example, in 1578 Saul was given the salt monopoly for all of Poland. While Saul was at the peak of his influence, the king of Poland died. The law said that the nobles must elect a new king on August 18, 1587. The nobles debated all day, and when they realized that it would be impossible to agree to elect a new king on the day prescribed by law, Prince Radziwill proposed they elect Saul Wahl until they could come to agreement.

The king had the power to make law, so in the short time Saul Wahl was king, he got busy enacting laws for the welfare of the Jews. One law provided that anyone who murdered a Jew should suffer the same penalty as if he had murdered a prince. The next day the nobles met once again and elected a new king, but Saul's laws stayed on the books.

Nine

THE AMERICAN REVOLUTION

The eastern seaboard of America has been settled for centuries, but it was once just a colony, ruled by another country, far away. During the summer of 1776, the Continental Congress decided it was time to declare their independence. In the context of its times, the document they produced was a radical one, in a time when kings still ruled virtually every country. When asked what they had produced during that hot Philadelphia summer in 1776, Benjamin Franklin replied, "A republic, if you can keep it."

Princess Diana
Philip Ahn
Irving Berlin
David Crosby
Cecil B. De Mille
Barbara Eden
Gloria Estefan
Tony Goldwyn

Goldie Hawn
Louis L'Amour
Gregory Peck
Anthony Perkins
Franklin Delano Roosevelt
Bette Davis
Katharine Hepburn
Jane Wyatt

Princess Diana

When Princess Diana's oldest son, Prince William, becomes king of England, England will have a king who is closely related to one of the greatest heroes of the American Revolution: Nathan Hale. General Washington asked for a volunteer to spy behind British lines. Nathan Hale, who arrived at the meeting late, stepped forward. Disguised as a schoolmaster, he was landed by armed sloop at Long Island and proceeded to study all the British troops'

PRINCESS DIANA

placements and prepare drawings of their military positions. Having accomplished his mission, he was arrested on his return after being searched by British sailors. He was immediately condemned to be hanged as a spy. The order was carried out the next morning—September 22, 1776—near the corner of Chambers and Centre Streets. His last words, which were to ring down through history, were, "I regret that I have but one life to give for my country."

Irving Berlin

Composer Irving Berlin was related, through his wife Ellin Travers MacKay, to Rufus King, a member of the Continental Congress, a member of the Constitutional Convention, a signer of the Constitution, and a member of the first Senate. In 1816 he ran for president against Monroe. In his bid for the presidency he was the last candidate of the Federalist party. His candidacy killed the party!

David Crosby

David Van Cortlandt Crosby, of the rock group Crosby, Stills, Nash and Young, is a direct descendant of William Floyd, a signer of the Declaration of Independence from New York. Floyd was an unsophisticated person who enjoyed the great estate on Long Island that he had inherited from his father. His days were spent riding to the hounds and hosting lavish parties. His job in the First Continental Congress was the only thing in his life he ever took seriously, and it cost him everything. The British looted his house, and his wife died in exile before the end of the war, never seeing her home again.

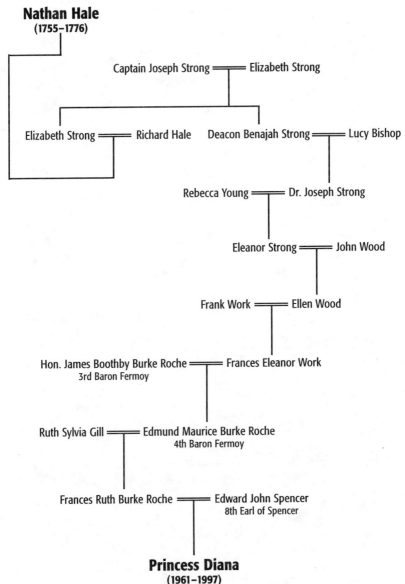

Nathan Hale
(1755–1776)

Captain Joseph Strong ══ Elizabeth Strong

Elizabeth Strong ══ Richard Hale

Deacon Benajah Strong ══ Lucy Bishop

Rebecca Young ══ Dr. Joseph Strong

Eleanor Strong ══ John Wood

Frank Work ══ Ellen Wood

Hon. James Boothby Burke Roche ══ Frances Eleanor Work
3rd Baron Fermoy

Ruth Sylvia Gill ══ Edmund Maurice Burke Roche
4th Baron Fermoy

Frances Ruth Burke Roche ══ Edward John Spencer
8th Earl of Spencer

Princess Diana
(1961–1997)

David Crosby is also descended from Dr. Ebenezer Crosby, George Washington's doctor during the Revolution, as well as Jacobus Van Cortlandt, a mayor of New York. David's father, Floyd Delafield Crosby, was a cinematographer for the great documentary filmmaker Robert Flaherty and worked with him on *White Shadows in the South Seas*.

Cecil B. De Mille

CECIL B. DE MILLE

Cecil Blount De Mille derived his middle name from his ancestor William Blount, who signed the U. S. Constitution for North Carolina. William Blount saw the American Revolution primarily as an opportunity to make money, and he made huge profits supplying the army. Elected to Congress, he never attended, considering the election an honor rather than a duty. After the war he engaged in land speculation in Tennessee, and when those speculations were jeopardized, he conspired with Aaron Burr to secede from the country, which gave him the dubious distinction of becoming the first U.S. Senator in the his-

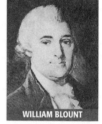

WILLIAM BLOUNT

tory of the country to be impeached. However, his larceny only increased his popularity in Tennessee, where he was elected president of the state senate.

Barbara Eden

BARBARA EDEN

Actress Barbara Eden is related to Benjamin Franklin, one of the chief architects of our country's freedom. Franklin first became famous with the publication of his *Poor Richard's Almanac*, in its day the best-known book in America. Rather than just giving the dull facts of the planting year, he delighted in including all sorts of sayings in the margins, such as, "Fish and visitors stink in three days." He was one of the five men who drafted the Declaration of Independence, and, at age 70, he was the oldest signer.

Franklin was sent to France as the American ambassador, where he played the part of the backwoods American to the hilt. In Philadelphia he had worn the latest Paris fashions, but in France he wore a coonskin cap. Once, at a Parisian literary society, Franklin couldn't follow the French and thus didn't know when to clap. So he followed the lead of everyone else, clapping when they clapped. When

BENJAMIN FRANKLIN

they left, his little grandson, who was much more fluent in French, said to him, "Grandpa, you shouldn't clap for yourself, it isn't polite."

Goldie Hawn

Actress Goldie Hawn, in her movie *Protocol*, reads the Declaration of Independence to a group of Middle Eastern diplomats, and then states: "That's the Declaration of Independence, we're really proud of that." What is not apparent in that scene is that Goldie is herself descended from John Rutledge, a

GOLDIE HAWN

JOHN RUTLEDGE

signer of the Declaration of Independence, and is closely related to five other signers of the Declaration and the Constitution. In honor of this ancestry, she named her son (whom she had with Bill Hudson of the Hudson Brothers, and who now has an acting career of his own) Oliver Rutledge Hudson. In Congress, when John Rutledge heard that the king had made some promises, he remarked, "I should have no regard for his word; his promises are not worth anything." After the war, John Rutledge was elected governor of Georgia. He chaired the committee that wrote the first draft of the Constitution and served as a justice on the U.S. Supreme Court.

Louis L'Amour

Louis Dearborn L'Amour is related to John Langdon, who was a delegate to the first Continental Congress, and who built ships for the new navy, including one for John Paul Jones. Langdon resigned from Congress to enter the army and fought in a number of Revolutionary battles, including the Battle of Bennington. After the war he was elected a member of the Constitutional Convention and signed the Constitution on behalf of New Hampshire.

Anthony Perkins

ANTHONY PERKINS

Actor Anthony Perkins is related to William Williams, a signer of the Declaration of Independence. William Williams spent his entire fortune in aid of the Revolution and then went from house to house asking for money to support the cause. When told by another delegate, "I am in no danger of being hung, for I have not signed the Declaration," Williams replied, "Then you deserve to be hung for not having done your duty!"

WILLIAM WILLIAMS

Franklin Delano Roosevelt

President Franklin Delano Roosevelt is related to the greatest traitor in American history, Benedict Arnold. Arnold started out as one of the United States' most brilliant generals, but he felt that his talents were to-

BENEDICT ARNOLD

tally unappreciated. Time and again he would win major battles, only to be criticized for little things. Fed up with Congress after they refused to make him commander in chief, he started listening to his new wife, Peggy, who had her sights set on being named Lady Arnold in the new province of America. After the war, living in England, he learned

FRANKLIN D. ROOSEVELT

a valuable lesson about life: nobody likes a traitor. When he asked for a command in the war against France, the earl of Louderdale made a speech against him in Parliament, calling him the very symbol of treachery. Arnold died an embittered man.

PATRIOTS OF THE AMERICAN REVOLUTION

The following celebrity ancestors fought in the American Revolution:

Orson Bean	Pvt. Asa Pollard (Massachusetts)
Joseph Cotten	Capt. Hudson Whitaker (North Carolina)
Richard Dix	Pvt. Jacob Brimmer (New York)
Robert Taylor	Ensign George Michael Spangler (Pennsylvania)
Shirley Temple	General William Amberson (Pennsylvania)
Ginger Rogers	Pvt. James McGrath (Pennsylvania)
John Lithgow	Major William Lithgow (Massachusetts)
Bing Crosby	Pvt. Enoch Crosby (Massachusetts)
John Wayne	Pvt. Isaac Buck, William Buck (Vermont)
Raymond Massey	Pvt. Jonathan Massey (Massachusetts)
Lee Marvin	Maj.Gen. Henry Lee (Virginia)
Steve McQueen	Pvt. Thomas McQueen (Maryland)
Carole Lombard	Pvt. Ralph Cheney (Maryland)
Brett Butler	General Nathaniel Greene (South Carolina)
General George S. Patton	General Hugh Mercer (Virginia)

Bette Davis and Katharine Hepburn

Both Bette Davis and Katharine Hepburn are related to John Hancock. On August 8, 1776, John Hancock, as president of the Continental Congress, was the first to sign the Declaration of Independence. After affixing his large signature to the document, he looked around at the nervous assembly, some of whom were reluctant to sign, and said, "We must all hang together." Benjamin Franklin, known for his wit, then replied, "We must all hang together, or certainly we shall all hang separately."

Jane Wyatt

Actress Jane Wyatt is descended from Phillip Livingston, who signed the Declaration of Independence, as well as William Paterson, who was born in Ireland, signed the Constitution as a representative from New Jersey, and had Paterson, New Jersey, named for him. She is also descended from Clement Moore, the man who wrote "The Night Before Christmas," and from Stephen Van Rensselaer, the last patroon of Rensselaerwyck, who founded Rensselaer Polytechnic College near Albany.

Orson Bean

Actor Orson Bean's maternal ancestry includes General Israel Putnam, a great hero of the American Revolution. Another ancestor was Asa Pollard, the first man killed at Bunker Hill. Pollard made the mistake, during the artillery bombardment of the American fortifications, of putting up his head to see what was going on. A cannonball, which was skipping along the ground, very neatly took it off.

Brett Butler

Comedienne Brett Butler, star of TV's *Grace Under Fire*, told the author at a luncheon that she is descended from General Nathaniel Greene, who commanded the entire southern army during the American Revolution, while Washington took command of the northern army. When Butler was a little girl, her parents placed her on a statue of General Greene in Charleston, South Carolina, and regaled her with stories of her illustrious ancestor.

Bing Crosby

Singer Bing Crosby's ancestor Enoch Crosby was a master spy during the Revolution. Posing as a Tory, he joined the British army and then sent valuable information to General Washington about the enemy's military movements. After the war Congress voted him a reward for his services, but he refused it, saying it was "not for gold that I served my country."

Lee Marvin

Actor Lee Marvin's ancestor, General Henry "Light Horse Harry" Lee, recruited a company of light cavalry at the beginning of the Revolution for Washington's army. He was quickly promoted to major for gallantry in battle and then captured a British fort at Powles Hook, New Jersey, in 1779, for which Congress voted him a gold medal. He was more than a match for Tarlton's Dragoons at Guilford Courthouse, aided in the capture of Forts Watson, Mott, and Granby, distinguished himself at Eutaw Springs, and was at Yorktown for the surrender of Lord Cornwallis. After the war Lee went into politics and was elected governor of Virginia. President Washington recalled him to active duty and appointed him a major general of the U.S. troops in 1794 to quell the Whiskey Rebellion, which arose because farmers were reluctant to pay taxes on their whiskey. Lee wrote and delivered the funeral oration for President Washington before both Houses of Congress, in which he uttered these famous words: "First in war, first in peace, and first in the hearts of his countrymen."

General George S. Patton

General George S. Patton was obsessed with the fact that he had two ancestors who died in battle as generals, and he must have been very disappointed to die in an auto accident. Patton was descended from General Hugh Mercer, who was with George Washington on General Edward Braddock's expedition and was killed during the American Revolution at the Battle of Princeton. His grandfather, also named General George S. Patton, commanded the 22nd Virginia Infantry, the only Confederate force to reach the city limits of Washington, D.C., during the Civil War, and he was killed at the third Battle of Winchester.

Robert Taylor

Actor Robert Taylor came into the world with a name that announced his ancestry in no uncertain terms: Spangler Arlington Brugh. His ancestor, George Michael Spangler, was an innkeeper in Warrington, York County, Pennsylvania, and upon the outbreak of the Revolution, served as an ensign in the 4th Company of the New Jersey Flying Camp in 1776.

PATRIOTS AROUND THE WORLD

Philip Ahn

Veteran character actor Philip Ahn's most famous role was as the "master" in the television series Kung Fu. His father, Chang Ho Ahn, was a great Korean patriot and national hero who opposed the Japanese long before the war and was murdered by them while being held in prison. Because of his father's death, Philip refused to play any Japanese parts during World War II, even though they were the majority of roles being offered to him.

Gloria Estefan

Singer Gloria Estefan was born in Havana, Cuba, and her father, Jose Manuel Fajardo, was a commander of the Exile Brigade, dedicated to liberating Cuba from the communists. With the encouragement of President Kennedy and the CIA, the Exile Brigade was trained and supplied with weapons and other military equipment, with the goal of invading Cuba. On April 17, 1961, the Exile Brigade landed at the Bay of Pigs. Jose Fajardo commanded the brigade's tank division. However, at the last minute President Kennedy refused to provide the air cover he had promised. Stranded on the beach, the Exile Brigade was on its own. Jose Manuel Fajardo was captured by his own cousin, who had taken Castro's

Shirley Temple

Actress Shirley Temple's ancestor is General William Amberson, who was an aide-de-camp to General Lafayette during the Revolution, and who later purchased large tracts of land at Fort Pitt, which is now known as Pittsburgh.

SHIRLEY TEMPLE

John Wayne

Actor John Wayne's 4th great-grandfather, Isaac Buck, fought and died with Ethan Allen and the Green Mountain Boys in the American attack on Montreal. His 3rd great-grandfather, William Buck, out to avenge his father, enlisted in the Revolutionary army at the age of 12.

side. It was only after eighteen months of suffering in prison that he was freed, when the U.S. shipped over $53 million worth of food and medicine to Cuba as ransom for the patriots. A career soldier, Fajardo joined the U.S. Army, rising quickly to the rank of captain in Vietnam.

Gregory Peck

Actor Gregory Peck is a cousin of Irish revolutionary Thomas Ashe. In 1916 Ashe led 400 Irish Volunteers in an ambush of the Royal Irish Constabulary, killing seven policemen and wounding fifteen. Then Ashe took part in the Easter Week rebellion. Captured during the fighting, he was tried by the British for murder and condemned to death by court-martial, but was reprieved by a general amnesty after a number of his comrades had already been executed. However, as a born rebel, it wasn't long before Ashe was arrested again, and this time he was sentenced to one year at hard labor for inciting to riot. He went on a hunger strike, and even though he was forcibly fed by the prison doctor, he died of starvation. His death was immediately exploited by the rebels. His coffin was draped in the Sinn Fein tricolor, and his funeral procession included a vast concourse of people, including the Lord Mayor of Dublin and the Roman Catholic archbishop of Dublin.

Franchot Tone

FRANCHOT TONE

Franchot Tone is related to Irish patriot and revolutionary leader Wolfe Tone. In 1788, Wolfe Tone went to France, where he convinced the Revolutionary government, at war with England, that an invasion of Ireland would be met with an uprising of the Irish people. He succeeded in putting together a large fleet, but was captured in the invasion. He was convicted of treason, but he killed himself before his captors could carry out the death sentence. Tone thus became a national hero and a symbol of Irish independence.

Ten

WITCHES AND WIZARDS

The people of Salem, Massachusetts, were terrified of witches and wizards. The witch hunt only lasted a few months, but by the time it was over, many innocent people had been executed.

Scientists have tried to determine the reason behind the witchcraft mania. One theory is that the crops that year were contaminated with the fungus *ergot*, whose chemical composition is lysergic acid amide, a close chemical cousin of LSD. If true, the whole witch episode was one bad trip.

In 1709 and 1750, the victims' next of kin unsuccessfully brought lawsuits against the colony of Massachusetts, not only for the loss of their loved ones, but also to clear their reputations. Two hundred and fifty years later, in 1957, more remote descendants finally succeeded in having a bill passed clearing their ancestors' names.

Walt Disney	≋	Wizard George Burroughs
Geena Davis	≋	Witch Rebecca Shelly
Lucille Ball	≋	Witch Sisters Rebecca Towne Nurse and Mary Towne Estey

John Wayne	≋	Witch Mary Bliss Parsons
Joan Kennedy	≋	Witch Mary Towne
Sir Winston Churchill	≋	Witch Mary Staples
Noah Webster	≋	Witch Lydia Gilbert

Noah Webster

NOAH WEBSTER

Noah Webster, a descendant of executed witch Lydia Gilbert, invented the dictionary. From the very first, his dictionary was a great success, selling like hotcakes, and Congress immediately adopted it as its official arbiter of the English language. Amazingly, it sold even better in England. No sooner did it become a best-seller than everyone began copying it, so Webster had to lobby the government to pass copyright laws (which didn't exist in 1790)! When Webster died, Charles and George Merriam bought the rights, and his book has remained the mainstay of their company every since.

As inventor of the dictionary, Noah Webster was never at a loss for words. Arriving home unexpectedly one day, Mrs. Webster was surprised to find Noah fooling around with their maid. She exclaimed, "Noah, I am *surprised!*" Letting go of the maid, Noah was quick to correct her. "No, my dear, it is I who am *surprised*, you are *astonished*."

Walt Disney

WALT DISNEY

Filmmaker Walt Disney's movies and Disneyland were influenced by the castles and witches in his own family history. On his father's side, aristocratic blood ran in his veins, and Sir Hugh Disney was a knight with a castle in Isigny-sur-Mer in Normandy, France. Although Walt Disney is best remembered for creating Mickey Mouse and Donald Duck, he also created a famous witch, Snow White's mother. Walt Disney is himself descended from the Reverend George Burroughs, the grand wizard of all the witches executed at Salem, Massachusetts.

When it came time to execute the Reverend Burroughs, all eyes were on him. As he stood on the gallows, he slowly, gravely, and faultlessly repeated the Lord's Prayer. Reciting the prayer was a brilliant and audacious stroke on his part. Popular belief held that a witch could not repeat the Lord's Prayer properly, since it was thought to be said backward at the witches' sabbath. If Burroughs had stammered, if he had so much as stopped to clear his throat, the crowd would have been sure he was guilty. His recitation haunted the spectators long afterwards, and people never stopped talking about the fact that Burroughs recited the Lord's Prayer that day. In everyone's mind, they had hanged an innocent man.

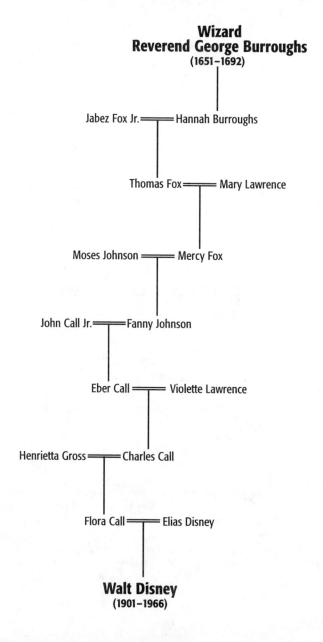

Wizard
Reverend George Burroughs
(1651–1692)

Jabez Fox Jr. ══ Hannah Burroughs

Thomas Fox ══ Mary Lawrence

Moses Johnson ══ Mercy Fox

John Call Jr. ══ Fanny Johnson

Eber Call ══ Violette Lawrence

Henrietta Gross ══ Charles Call

Flora Call ══ Elias Disney

Walt Disney
(1901–1966)

Eleven
WILD WEST

The western was already a staple of American life before the arrival of the movies, as a result of Buffalo Bill's Wild West Show and the penny novel. Some of its personalities, such as Wyatt Earp, were even consultants on movies about themselves! As late as the 1960s, when Hollywood made *Butch Cassidy and the Sundance Kid*, Butch's sister was on the set as a technical advisor about her outlaw brother.

Tom Selleck	≋	Buffalo Bill
George Bush	≋	Wild Bill Hickok
Cole Younger	≋	Chief Justice John Marshall
Wallis Simpson, Duchess of Windsor	≋	Jesse James
David Canary	≋	Calamity Jane

George Bush

Two frustrated baseball players are linked together by blood—Wild Bill Hickok and his cousin, President George Bush. Hickok's time in Kansas City was not entirely spent playing poker with Wyatt Earp, Bat Masterson, and Doc Holliday. Much more important in his life was baseball; Hickok was a diehard fan of the Kansas City Antelopes. You can well imagine that baseball was somewhat different in the Wild West. When the home team, the Antelopes, had an unfavorable ruling from the umpire, that umpire

GEORGE BUSH

might find his life in danger. The crowd was apt to look for a rope and lynch him, or one of the excited fans might just accidentally shoot him. This really made it difficult to finish a game and, ultimately, impossible to find an umpire—until the town finally voted Wild Bill into the job. When Wild Bill stood behind home plate,

WILD BILL HICKOK

wearing matching six-guns, the crowd was under control for the first time in the history of Kansas City baseball.

Wallis Simpson, Duchess of Windsor

WALLIS SIMPSON

Wallis Simpson may have stolen the heart of the king of England, but she was hardly a bandit like her famous cousin Jesse James. In order to marry Wallis Simpson, the former King Edward VIII had to abdicate his throne. Edward was once asked how he kept up his domestic bliss. "All you have to do," he remarked, "is to remind your wife that you gave up the throne of England for her. It usually shuts her up."

JESSE JAMES

Ironically, Jesse James has descendants who are lawmen. Jesse's son, Jesse James Jr., was a lawyer, and his great-grandson James R. Ross is a Superior Court judge in Orange County, California. As James Ross said, "He always said he had a built-in clientele as a defense attorney. What criminal wouldn't trust Jesse James Jr. as his lawyer?"

Tom Selleck

The word in actor Tom Selleck's family is that he is related to Buffalo Bill Cody, the creator of the Wild West show and the inspiration for the movie business's fascination with the West. Bill started his career as a rider on the Pony Express, answering an advertisement which read, "Wanted: Young, skinny, wiry fellows not over 18. Must be expert riders willing to risk death daily. Orphans preferred."

TOM SELLECK

Dalton and Younger Gangs

JOHN MARSHALL

In a strange twist of fate, the Dalton Gang and the Younger Gang, who were first cousins, were related to John Marshall, the most famous chief justice of the U.S. Supreme Court. Cole Younger was so proud of his relationship to Marshall that it was the first thing he mentioned in his autobiography.

Life on the Supreme Court was different in those days. In the argument of *Fletcher v. Peck*, John Marshall was forced to adjourn the court so that one of the justices could sober up sufficiently to understand the arguments. At one point the drinking in court became such a scandal that Marshall decreed that they could only drink on the bench if it was raining. The next day, as they sat through one boring brief after another, Marshall kept sending justices to the window to see if it was raining. Finally, in desperation, Marshall declared, "The jurisdiction of this court extends throughout the country, and it must be raining somewhere. Get me a drink."

COLE YOUNGER

The Daltons flew into national prominence as a result of the Coffeyville raid. Fifteen minutes after they rode into town, four of the gang were dead and the fifth pretty badly shot up. Bill Dalton, who had not been on the Coffeyville raid, had a lot of gall. He wrote to Coffeyville from his ranch in California that his brother Emmett was carrying $900 when they rode into town that day. A careful accounting revealed that there was indeed $900 in excess of the amount lost! Emmett Dalton later moved to Hollywood, where he became a technical expert on outlaws, including a film about himself and his brothers entitled *When the Daltons Rode*.

David Canary

Emmy Award-winning soap star of *All My Children*, David Canary also played the role of Candy on TV's *Bonanza*, taking the place of the departed Pernel Roberts in the cast. Canary claims to be related to Martha Jane Canary, better known as Calamity Jane. Calamity Jane hoped that her connection to Wild Bill would help her break into show business. (She claimed they had married.) In 1895, Calamity Jane had some 8–by–10 glossies made up, in the hopes that it would convince a Wild West show to hire her. When that didn't work, she printed a booklet entitled *The Life and Adventures of Calamity Jane by Herself*. At the Pan American Exposition of 1901, she rented a booth and stood on the midway trying to sell it. However, her show business career never materialized.

In the 1930s, a woman claimed to be the long-lost daughter of Calamity Jane and Wild Bill. Even though her story was discredited, the publicity renewed interest in Calamity Jane, leading to a string of films starring Jane Russell, Jean Arthur, and even a musical version of her life with Doris Day!

Iron Eyes Cody

Character actor Iron Eyes Cody is best known as the Indian crying a single tear in the "Keep America Beautiful" ad campaign. His father, Thomas Longplume Cody, toured with Buffalo Bill's Wild West show as an expert horseman and trick rider. Buffalo Bill, whose last name was also Cody, felt that one Cody in the show wasn't enough! Iron Eyes' grandfather, a Cherokee named Randolph Abshire Cody, was an outlaw. During the Civil War, he joined Quantrill's Raiders, who would burn whole towns in Kansas and Missouri and kill everyone in them. Like many Confederate guerrillas, after the war he kept up his outlaw ways, sticking up stagecoaches and trains. Because his gang was comprised of four Indians and one black man, his wild bunch never became famous, a privilege reserved for white desperadoes.

Gary Cooper

Actor Gary Cooper's uncle Walter Cooper was inspired to come to Montana from Houghton Regis, in Bedfordshire, England, by news of the massacre of General George Armstrong Custer at Little Bighorn. He had planned on becoming an Indian fighter, but by the time he arrived the

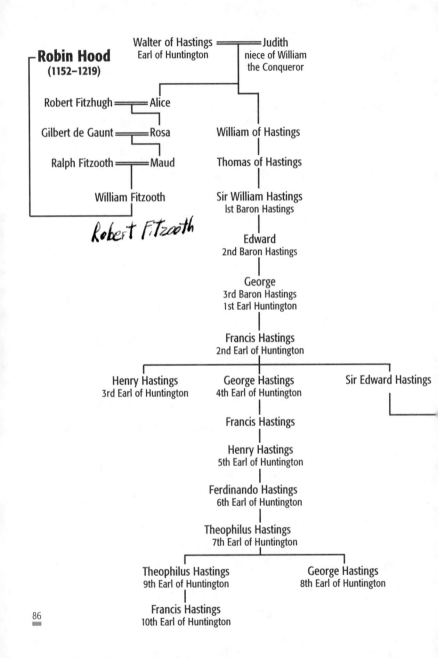

Robin Hood
(1152–1219)

Walter of Hastings ══════ Judith
Earl of Huntington   niece of William
                           the Conqueror

Robert Fitzhugh ══════ Alice

Gilbert de Gaunt ══════ Rosa

Ralph Fitzooth ══════ Maud

William Fitzooth

Robert Fitzooth

William of Hastings

Thomas of Hastings

Sir William Hastings
1st Baron Hastings

Edward
2nd Baron Hastings

George
3rd Baron Hastings
1st Earl Huntington

Francis Hastings
2nd Earl of Huntington

Henry Hastings   George Hastings   Sir Edward Hastings
3rd Earl of Huntington   4th Earl of Huntington

Francis Hastings

Henry Hastings
5th Earl of Huntington

Ferdinando Hastings
6th Earl of Huntington

Theophilus Hastings
7th Earl of Huntington

Theophilus Hastings   George Hastings
9th Earl of Huntington   8th Earl of Huntington

Francis Hastings
10th Earl of Huntington

ROBIN HOOD ≈ PATRICK MACNEE

PATRICK MACNEE

The Younger Gang thought of themselves as modern-day Robin Hoods; they would take from the rich—in this case, the rich railroad—and give money to their poor neighbors, who naturally did everything they could to help them hide from the sheriff.

A present-day descendant of legendary outlaw Robin Hood is Patrick Macnee, the star of the popular 1960s television show *The Avengers*. The Robin Hood legend came to America with the first immigrants, and from the silent masterpiece *Robin Hood*, with Douglas Fairbanks, to the classic *The Adventures of Robin Hood*, with Errol Flynn, right up to *Robin Hood, Prince of Thieves*, with Kevin Costner, Robin Hood has always been a popular character for feature films.

Robin Hood was actually Robert, earl of Huntington, a nobleman who fought the sheriff of Nottingham under the name of Robin Hood. The earls of Huntington have always been proud of this connection and have repeatedly used Robin Hood as middle names for their children.

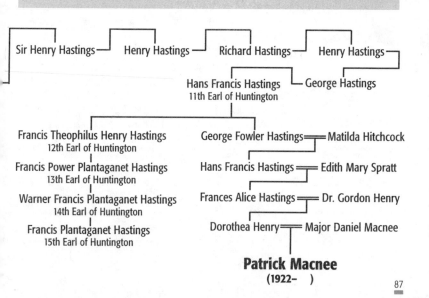

Sir Henry Hastings — Henry Hastings — Richard Hastings — Henry Hastings —

Hans Francis Hastings
11th Earl of Huntington — George Hastings

Francis Theophilus Henry Hastings
12th Earl of Huntington

Francis Power Plantaganet Hastings
13th Earl of Huntington

Warner Francis Plantaganet Hastings
14th Earl of Huntington

Francis Plantaganet Hastings
15th Earl of Huntington

George Fowler Hastings══Matilda Hitchcock

Hans Francis Hastings ══ Edith Mary Spratt

Frances Alice Hastings══Dr. Gordon Henry

Dorothea Henry══Major Daniel Macnee

Patrick Macnee
(1922–)

Indian wars were over. His letters home were still encouraging enough to induce his brother Charles, Gary Cooper's father, to emigrate as well. Charles studied law, and in the 1920s he became a justice on the Montana Supreme Court.

Fiorello La Guardia

Three-term New York City mayor Fiorello La Guardia is thought by many, because of his great love for the city, to be a native New Yorker, but he didn't arrive there until he was twenty-three years old. He was brought up on the western frontier! His father, Achille La Guardia, was a regimental bandmaster in the U.S. Army, and Fiorello spent his youth at remote army outposts in the West, which explains why he would often be seen around New York in a Stetson hat. His early exposure to crooked Indian agents gave him a strong aversion to corruption. Today he is remembered for racing to fires, smashing slot machines, and reading the funny papers to children over the radio during the newspaper strike.

Lee Meriwether

Actress Lee Meriwether is related to western explorer Meriwether Lewis of the Lewis and Clark Expedition. A mystery surrounds the circumstances of Meriwether Lewis's death even today. While traveling to Washington he stopped at a wayside inn. The account of the innkeeper's wife attests that he was deranged and shot himself in the head with his pistol. However, the money he was carrying with him was never found, and that threw suspicion on the innkeeper and his wife. When questioned, they changed their story, stating that Lewis's servant was seen wearing his master's clothes and had probably made off with the money. But the servant died under mysterious circumstances before he could be questioned, throwing suspicion back on the innkeeper, who disappeared, presumably with the money!

Joel McCrea

Actor Joel McCrea's grandfather, Major John M. McCrea, fought with General Phineas Banning against the Apaches and later established a stagecoach line in California. His maternal grandfather, Major Albert Whipple, came west on a wagon train and established a hotel in San Francisco.

JOHN WAYNE, AMERICAN

JOHN WAYNE

John Wayne (alias Marion Morrison) didn't have to look far into his own ancestry to find role models for his many western characters. His roots demonstrate why the memorial gold medal awarded by Congress after his death simply says, "John Wayne, American."

The number of John Wayne's ancestors that he portrayed in films is legion, and it's easy to see that his whole screen persona is merely a reflection of his ancestry. For example, the film *In Old California* was a tribute to his father, Clyde Morrison, in which Wayne played a frontier pharmacist, his father's profession. His grandfather Robert E. Brown was an old Indian fighter who told stories of his exploits to his young grandson, who thought his grandpa was an expert on everything.

His paternal ancestor, Judge Robert Morrison, had been a member of the United Irishmen. He fled his native country in the face of political reprisal and settled in Ohio, where he became a member of the militia, a self-taught judge, and was elected to the legislature. He was later appointed a brigadier gener-

PATRICK WAYNE

al by his friend President William Henry Harrison. Marion Mitchell Morrison, for whom John Wayne was named, was shot in the head during the Civil War and left for dead, but survived to tell the tale to his grandson. John Wayne is even related to that all-American hero Johnny Appleseed, who wandered around the Ohio River valley carrying apple seeds that he used to start apple trees throughout the frontier. With ancestors like that, it would have been impossible for John Wayne to be anything but the man he was: "John Wayne, American."

Chester A. Nimitz

The grandfather of naval hero Chester A. Nimitz, the commander in chief of the Pacific Fleet during World War II, was Carl Heinrich Nimitz, a Texas Ranger. Farther back on the family tree is Major General Ernest von Nimitz of the Swedish army, who fought against the Poles at Warsaw in 1656, took part in the campaign at Fredericka, and was taken prisoner in 1658 at the Battle of Kronenberg.

Fay Wray

Actress Fay Wray, best known as the star of *King Kong*, is the great-grand-daughter of Philander Colton, a soldier who served with the Mormon Battalion during the Mexican War. This battalion was raised in Utah and then sent on a long march to California to capture San Diego for the United States. A monument stands in San Diego today to honor their expedition. Fay Wray's grandfather Daniel Webster Jones also fought in the war. While in Mexico, he became fond of the people and learned to read and write Spanish. After his discharge, he was en route to California with a trading company when he was injured and had to be left behind. Mormons nursed him back to health, and this led him to translate the Book of Mormon into Spanish for Brigham Young.

Peter Lawford and Steve Young

Actor Peter Lawford and football star Steve Young are both related to Brigham Young, an early convert to the Mormon religion who became so zealous that he was soon second in command to founder Joseph Smith. When Smith was murdered by a mob

PETER LAWFORD

in 1844, Brigham became the new head of the church. As persecution drove them from town to town, he oversaw

BRIGHAM YOUNG

their migration west to the valley of the Great Salt Lake. When Utah entered the union, he was the first governor, and through his many wives he left a progeny of fifty-six children. The largest university in Utah now bears his name.

Twelve

AUTHOR! AUTHOR!

◎◎

Robert Duvall	William Shakespeare
Mike Myers	William Wordsworth
Robby Van Winkle, aka Vanilla Ice	Rip Van Winkle
F. Scott Fitzgerald	Francis Scott Key
Jean Harlow	Edgar Allan Poe
Margaux and Mariel Hemingway	Elihu Yale, Ernest Hemingway
James Dean	John Greenleaf Whittier
John Derek	Mark Twain
Geraldine Chaplin	Eugene O'Neill
O. Henry	Aaron Burr
Laura Dern	Archibald MacLeish
George Plimpton	Emily Dickinson
Lee Remick	Ralph Waldo Emerson
June Lockhart	Sir Walter Scott
Jane Wyatt	Clement Moore
Dan Quayle	Henry Wadsworth Longfellow
Dr. Benjamin Spock	Ralph Waldo Emerson
Lucille Ball	Robert Frost
Daniel Day-Lewis	Cecil Day-Lewis, Poet Laureate of England

Mike Myers

Comedian Mike Myers, whose film credits include *Wayne's World* and *Austin Powers*, is related to William Wordsworth, poet laureate of England in 1843, and considered the greatest poet of the nineteenth century.

The poet was as bizarre as his famous descendant. He was a great supporter of the French Revolution, which was not very popular in his native England, where the king wanted to stay on the throne. But then Wordsworth went to France, immediately abandoning his radical politics when he fell in love with a beautiful French girl who was against the Revolution. He never married the French girl, however, preferring his incestuous relationship with his sister Dorothy, with whom he collaborated on a number of works. When he married a childhood friend, Dorothy couldn't bear to go the wedding; she just stayed home and cried for days.

Robert Duvall

Robert Duvall has had a number of movie roles in which he has played military men, such as *The Great Santini*, and the accuracy he brings to these roles makes sense when you realize that his father, William Howard Duvall, graduated from Annapolis and retired as a rear admiral. (Actress Shelley Duvall is a descendant of the same French Huguenot family that settled in Virginia.)

Perhaps Robert Duvall's most interesting ancestor from a creative standpoint is the very Bard of Avon himself, William Shakespeare. People often ask where the author gets all of this great information, and this little tidbit of genealogical lore was actually conveyed to the author personally by Robert Duvall at a Beverly Hills eatery.

Robby Van Winkle (Vanilla Ice)

Rapper Vanilla Ice (Robby Van Winkle) is descended from the Van Winkle family of New York, and is related to the original Rip Van Winkle. When Washington Irving was writing his famous story, he based the name of his character on that of his printer, Cornelius Van Winkle, whom he called "Old Rip."

As a printer, Rip Van Winkle had published a number of Washington Irving's books, and he knew Irving was not known for delivering his manuscripts on time. Even though the story had already been set in type, Washington Irving had not yet settled on a name for his hero. Cornelius insisted that Irving make up his mind, because he needed to use the type for printing other books. Irving exclaimed in desperation, "Well, Old Rip, it will be Rip . . . Rip Van Winkle!"

Jean Harlow

JEAN HARLOW AND
JEAN POE HARLOW

Platinum-blond bombshell Jean Harlow was related through her mother, Jean Poe Harlow, to the short story expert Edgar Allan Poe.

Most people don't know that Poe was expelled from West Point. Regulations required cadets to appear in parade dress uniform, including white belts and gloves. He appeared for public parade wearing those items, but nothing else, and unfortunately his rifle did not cover his gun.

Poe's 1831 tale, *The Murder of Marie Roget,* was based on the real murder of Mary Cecilia Rogers in New York City, which so shocked the city that it decided to start a police force in 1841. The new police force was issued copper stars, which gave rise to their nickname "cops."

EDGAR ALLAN POE

Margaux and Mariel Hemingway

Actresses Margaux and Mariel Hemingway are the granddaughters of author Ernest Hemingway. When Hemingway won the Nobel Prize for literature in 1954, he was introduced to the previous American winner, William Faulkner, who said, "Ernest, you never use a word that might send the reader to the dictionary."

The Hemingways' ancestor Elihu Yale was born in America, the grandson of Theophilus Eaton, who with the Reverend John Davenport (my ancestor), founded the colony at New Haven. Yale eventually ended up, around the year 1700, in India, where he rose to become the rather despotic governor of Madras. Not a nice guy, he hanged his groom for taking a three-day holiday without having accrued sufficient vacation time. He was eventually relieved of his job by the East India Company, and when he returned to England he is credited with having invented the auction to sell off the large amount of goods he brought back from his adventures. As a gentleman of means in England, he was constantly approached for handouts, and the little school in New Haven was no exception. Rather than just begging for money, the school's founders hit upon a better scheme. They pointed out to him that the best monument that a man could leave behind was to have his name on a school. They then proceeded to tell him how much it was going to cost to have this everlasting monument, and he paid up.

James Dean

JAMES DEAN

Actor James Dean was related to poet John Greenleaf Whittier. Whittier, although he grew up on the frontier, was never harmed by the Indians because he was a Quaker. Raiding parties would kill his neighbors, but never have more than a friendly greeting for him. At one point they massacred forty people in the nearby town. As the war party rode by his house, their hands red with blood and the scalps dangling from their belts still dripping, they waved to Whittier.

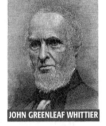

JOHN GREENLEAF WHITTIER

John Derek

Producer John Derek was a relative of author Mark Twain, who, if he were alive today, would probably have a string of sitcoms. Once, Mark Twain's wife came into the living room and discovered him howling with laughter over a book. She asked him what he was reading, and when he didn't know the title, she looked at the cover to discover he was reading one of his own books!

When Twain was in London, a rumor of his imminent death reached the editor of the *New York Journal*, who telegraphed, "If Mark Twain dying in poverty in London send 500 words, if Mark Twain has died in poverty send 1,000 words." Mark Twain wired back, "The report of my death is greatly exaggerated."

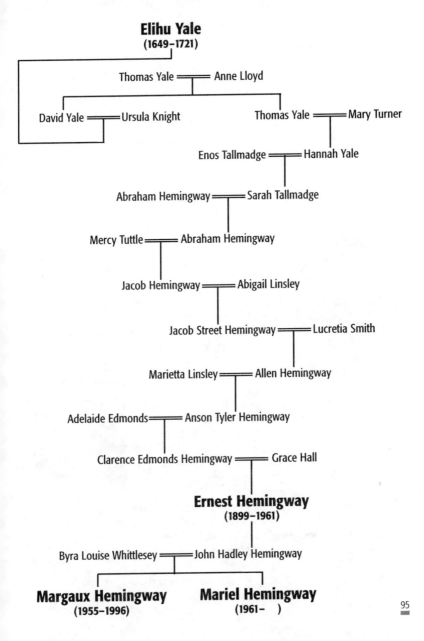

Elihu Yale
(1649–1721)

Thomas Yale ══ Anne Lloyd

David Yale ══ Ursula Knight

Thomas Yale ══ Mary Turner

Enos Tallmadge ══ Hannah Yale

Abraham Hemingway ══ Sarah Tallmadge

Mercy Tuttle ══ Abraham Hemingway

Jacob Hemingway ══ Abigail Linsley

Jacob Street Hemingway ══ Lucretia Smith

Marietta Linsley ══ Allen Hemingway

Adelaide Edmonds ══ Anson Tyler Hemingway

Clarence Edmonds Hemingway ══ Grace Hall

Ernest Hemingway
(1899–1961)

Byra Louise Whittlesey ══ John Hadley Hemingway

Margaux Hemingway
(1955–1996)

Mariel Hemingway
(1961–)

Geraldine Chaplin

Geraldine Chaplin, the daughter of Charlie Chaplin and his wife, Oona O'Neill, played her own grandmother in the film *Chaplin*. Charlie Chaplin once entered a Charlie Chaplin look-alike competition in the city of Monte Carlo. He came in third.

Not only is Geraldine the daughter of Charlie Chaplin, but she is also the granddaughter of playwright Eugene O'Neill. Eugene O'Neill won a Pulitzer Prize for his first play, *Beyond the Horizon*, and in 1936 received the Nobel Prize for literature. O'Neill was reluctant to cut any words from his plays. When they insisted he take fifteen minutes out of *Ah, Wilderness!* he replied, "Get rid of the intermission."

O. Henry

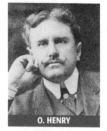

O. HENRY

Author O. Henry is related to Aaron Burr, the only vice president ever tried for treason. O. Henry is best known for amusing stories with surprise endings, fifty years before Rod Serling made the format popular with *The Twilight Zone*. His most popular story is "The Gift of the Magi," in which a young husband sells his watch to buy a comb for his wife's hair, and she sells her hair to buy a chain for her husband's watch.

O. Henry didn't start out to be a writer. He was a bank teller until the bank discovered he was short on the accounts, at which point he immediately fled the country to Honduras. Learning that his wife was ill, he returned to her side, only to watch her die. As a result, O. Henry was caught and during his five years in the federal penitentiary, he discovered he

AARON BURR

was a writer! Once, O. Henry wrote his publisher requesting an advance, even though he was already in arrears. The publisher refused to give him any money unless he knew what it was for. He received by return post an envelope with a single blond hair. Henry got the advance.

Aaron Burr, irritated that he wasn't elected president and blaming Alexander Hamilton for it, killed him in a duel, thus becoming the only vice president to be indicted for murder. As a result, he was not nominated to run again. Disgusted, he devised a scheme to split off part of the United States, with him as president, and he narrowly escaped a hangman's noose for treason. Luckily, the man who presided over his trial, Chief Justice John Marshall, hated Jefferson, and ran the trial in a manner guaranteed to acquit Burr. Burr then went to France and proposed to Napoleon that he finance an expedition to conquer Louisiana and Canada, but the emperor turned him down flat.

Laura Dern

Actress Laura Dern is the great-grandniece of author Archibald MacLeish through her father, actor Bruce Dern, and she is a cousin to playwright Tennessee Williams through her mother, actress Diane Ladd. Pulitzer Prize-winning author Archibald MacLeish was appointed Librarian of Congress by President

LAURA DERN

Franklin Roosevelt, a controversial appointment considering the fact that he knew absolutely nothing about being a librarian, and the American Library Association sent a long letter of protest. In his defense he stated, "I have written a lot of books." Tennessee Williams, one of the greatest twentieth-century playwrights, whose plays explore what he called "the unlighted side" of human nature, won Pulitzer Prizes for *A Streetcar Named Desire* and *Cat On A Hot Tin Roof*.

BRUCE DERN

George Plimpton

Author George Plimpton is related to Emily Dickinson, one of the most sexually repressed and brilliant poets in American literary history. She never ventured beyond her parents' house and garden, she never married, and her only romantic relationships were in her own mind. Her thoughts are revealed through her poetry. One of her poems begins, "Wild Nights — Wild Nights, Were I with thee, Wild Nights should be!" Most biographers attribute her flood of creativity to her unrequited love for several men, including a married minister by the name of Mr. Charles Wadsworth. She obtained pictures of him from friends, and she dressed all in white in homage. In her letters to her "Master," she invited him to visit her and promised that he would not be disappointed!

Tennessee Williams

TENNESSEE WILLIAMS

Tennessee Williams, famous American dramatist, had to admit he was not born in Tennessee. However, in his own defense, he remarked that he was a direct descendant of the first senator from Tennessee, John Williams. He was also descended from Valentine Sevier, the brother of Tennessee's first governor, John Sevier, and from Thomas Lanier Williams, first chancellor for the Western Territory, which was what Tennessee was called before it became a state. As he explains it, "In naming myself, I just indulged in the Southern weakness for climbing the family tree."

Dan Quayle

DAN QUAYLE

You would think that vice president Dan Quayle would have been a better speller, considering his blood relationship to literary giant Henry Wadsworth Longfellow. There is no record of Longfellow ever misspelling the word "potato."

In the popular culture, Longfellow is best known for his poems "Evangeline,"

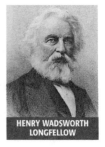
HENRY WADSWORTH LONGFELLOW

"Hiawatha," and "The Courtship of Myles Standish." The latter was inspired by the fact that he was directly descended from that famous Puritan couple, John Alden and Priscilla Mullins, and was just reciting his own family history when he wrote the tale of America's first love triangle.

Dr. Benjamin Spock

Dr. Benjamin Spock, pediatrician, baby doctor, and peace advocate, is related to Ralph Waldo Emerson (as is actress Lee Remick). An established pediatrician, Spock got into the baby business during World War II when a friend suggested that he write a book on raising children. Contrary to other child development theories prevalent at the time, he advocated a more relaxed method of child rearing. His timing could not have been better. With the end of the war, the baby boom hit and sales skyrocketed.

Lucille Ball

Leave it to Lucy to have the final word! It recently came to light that Lucy had written her autobiography in the early 1960s and publishers scrambled to get their hands on it! The 312–page memoir lay, forgotten, until an old photocopy was found in the personal effects of her deceased publicity director, Howard McClay. The famous comedienne is related to writer Robert Frost, whose father's Confederate leanings were so pronounced that he named his son Robert E. Lee Frost.

Young Robert Frost was a trial to his parents; he dropped out of both Dartmouth and Harvard without receiving his degree, preferring to work at odd jobs and write poetry. His grandfather, in an attempt to make an honest citizen out of him, bought him a farm in New Hampshire, but Frost was an eccentric farmer, milking his cows late at night so that he would not have to get up early in the morning.

With his newfound fame Frost became a professor, a strange fate for a man who could not stand higher education and who flunked out of college twice. On one occasion, a student asked him to explain one of his poems. His reply was Frosty: "What do you want me to do, rewrite it in bad English?"

William Wyler

Famed film director William Wyler, the great-nephew of novelist Bertold Auerback, was brought to America by his cousin Carl Laemmle, who was running Universal Studios and populating almost the entire studio with his European relatives. Carl Laemmle must have had a slightly different set of genes from his bright relatives Wyler and Auerback. Laemmle once hired a writer from Australia. He asked him how long he had been in America, and when the writer replied two weeks, Carl remarked, "It's amazing how well you speak English after only two weeks!"

June Lockhart

Actress June Lockhart, through her father, actor Gene Lockhart, claims on

who married Lockhart's eldest daughter. Lockhart first published his biography of Scott in seven volumes, and later expanded it into a ten-volume edition in 1839. Because Sir Walter died deep in debt, Lockhart turned all of the profits from the book over to Scott's creditors. His eldest son, John Hugh Lockhart, was the Hugh Little John of Scott's *Tales of a Grandfather*.

William Inge

Distinguished playwright William Inge was a relative of actor John Wilkes Booth, the man who shot Abraham Lincoln.

Grace Kelly

Grace Kelly, the beautiful American actress who married into royalty, thereby becoming the princess of Monaco, was the niece of George Kelly, who received a Pulitzer Prize for his play *Craig's Wife*. Grace Kelly was also the daughter of John Brendan Kelly Sr., the holder of two Olympic gold medals and probably the greatest single sculler the world has ever known.

GRACE KELLY

Daniel Day-Lewis

DANIEL DAY-LEWIS

Actor Daniel Day-Lewis is the son of Cecil Day-Lewis, poet laureate of England and the creator, under the pen name Nicholas Blake, of the detective Nigel Strangeways featured in over twenty novels.

Daniel's mother is actress Jill Balcon, the daughter of film producer Sir Michael Balcon. Michael Balcon began producing films after World War I and founded Gainsborough Pictures, making films with Alfred Hitchcock. He also backed documentary director Robert J. Flaherty. Becoming the head of production at Ealing Studios, he built up that studio during World War II, and after the war produced a string of comedies with Alec Guinness.

Thirteen

CAPTAINS OF INDUSTRY AND INVENTION

Whether it's building a better mouse trap or selling it, that's where the money is. Creativity in show business can spring from creativity in almost any type of endeavor, and selling yourself is just like selling anything else.

Charles Darwin	Josiah Wedgwood
Patty Hearst	William Randolph Hearst
Chevy Chase	Cornelius Vanderbilt Crane
Carole Lombard	Gentleman Jim Cheney
Michael Eisner	Milton Dammann
Hume Cronyn	John Kinder Labatt
Ted Field	Marshall Field
Gloria Vanderbilt	Cornelius Vanderbilt
Spencer Tracy	Nicholas Brown, Founder of Brown University
Tuesday Weld	Eli Whitney
Linda Ronstadt	Lloyd Groff Copeman, Inventor of the Rubber Ice Cube Tray
Ann Sothern	Simon Lake, Inventor of the Submarine
Norman Rockwell	Alfonso Rockwell, Inventor of the Electric Chair
Olivia Newton-John	Nobel Prize Winner Max Born

Lizzie Borden

LIZZIE BORDEN

Gail Borden and Lizzie Borden make an unlikely pair of cousins: one made ice cold milk, the other was a cold-blooded killer.

Gail Borden got the idea for his evaporated milk from the Shakers, who used vacuum pans to concentrate fruit juice. The pans, with no air inside, would allow the liquid to evaporate at a lower temperature. However, Borden had to compete with "swill milk," a ghastly combination of milk, water, chalk, and molasses that the good citizens of New York City thought was great. It was only when Borden cleverly planted a newspaper story, "the truth about swill milk," that he was able to take over the milk market.

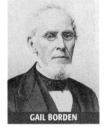

GAIL BORDEN

Lizzie Borden has been immortalized in the famous children's rhyme, "Lizzie Borden took an ax, and gave her mother forty wacks. When her father saw what she'd done, she gave her father forty-one." After a notorious trial, she was acquitted, and lived to have many descendants of her own, none of whom seem to have inherited her penchant for killing their parents.

Charles Darwin

Evolutionist Charles Darwin was not only the grandson of poet Erasmus Darwin, but also of pottery king Josiah Wedgwood. Prior to Wedgwood, dinner was normally served in one communal bowl, with each family member digging into the common morass. His development of a method of assembly-line glazing allowed each person at dinner to have his own plate. He was soon in such demand that the queen of England herself came to him, and he capitalized on this by bringing out a line of plates called "Queen's Ware." For the first time in history, there could be such a thing as table etiquette!

Patty Hearst

Celebrity hostage Patty Hearst is the great-granddaughter of newspaper and mining tycoon William Randolph Hearst, the inspiration for Orson

PATTY HEARST

Welles's film *Citizen Kane*. Just as in *Citizen Kane*, Hearst started the Spanish-American War almost single-handedly with his newspaper. He sent artist Frederic Remington to Cuba to cover the revolution, but Remington couldn't find one. Hearst wired back, "You furnish the pictures, I'll furnish the war." Hearst printed every story of Spanish atrocities, no matter how unreliable. His newspaper's campaign notwithstanding, it was only when the U.S. battleship *Maine* mysteriously blew up in Havana harbor that Hearst got his war. Quick to capitalize on it, he created a card game called War with Spain, and his

WILLIAM RANDOLPH HEARST

next headline read, "How do you like the *Journal*'s war?" To top it off, he offered his readers a thousand-dollar prize for the best idea on how to get the war off to a good start.

Chevy Chase

Comedian Chevy Chase, whose real name is Cornelius Crane Chase, was named by his mother after her stepfather Cornelius Vanderbilt Crane, for whom she had great affection. Cornelius Vanderbilt Crane was the heir to the Crane Plumbing Company, founded by his grandfather, Richard Teller Crane. Crane is a name that most men in America will recognize from standing in front of a urinal.

Chevy is also related, through his maternal great-grandmother, Charlotte Margaret Linné, to Carl von Linné (Linnaeus), the founder of modern botany. Linnaeus designed the method of biological classification which is still in use today, in which organisms are repeatedly subdivided and classified according to their class, genus, and species.

Michael Eisner

Walt Disney successor Michael Dammann Eisner, now most sincerely rich, worked his way up from being merely rich. His great-grandfather Sigmund Eisner made a fortune in the garment industry, and Sigmund's son, Lester Eisner, who styled himself Colonel Eisner, increased the fortune. Lester Jr. attended Harvard Law School where he learned you can have even more money if you marry into it, so he married Margaret Dammann, the daughter of Milton Dammann, one of the founders of the American Safety Razor Company, which later became part of Philip Morris.

Hume Cronyn

Actor Hume Cronyn's great-uncle, Edward Blake, was premier of Ontario and a member of the Canadian Parliament. After several defeats on his policies, Blake switched to the British Parliament, where he advocated the cause of the Irish independence. Probably of more interest to the beer-drinking mass of Americans is the fact that Hume Cronyn is also descended from John Kinder Labatt, who founded the brewery which bears his name.

Ted Field

Ted Field, producer of almost 50 films, including *Mr. Holland's Opus, The Hand That Rocks the Cradle, Cocktail,* and *Three Men and a Baby*, is the son of Marshall Field IV and a direct descendant of Marshall Field, the merchandising genius who created one of the largest chains of retail stores in the world. An innovator, Field was the first to offer gift wrapping, to establish a "bargain basement," and to open a restaurant in the store. He coined the motto, "The customer is always right."

Gloria Vanderbilt

Clothing designer Gloria Vanderbilt is a direct descendant of one of the most famous of the nineteenth-century robber barons, Cornelius Vanderbilt. The mogul started out with one boat and built his business into a great shipping empire. Cornelius Vanderbilt hated railroads because in 1833 he had been badly injured, along with former president John Quincy Adams, in the first train wreck in history. It was not until the 1860s, when everyone else was making a fortune from railroads that he finally got over his prejudice and got into the business. He soon gained a monopoly, and when he died in 1877, he was worth $104 million, $2 million more than was in the U.S. Treasury at the time. Cornelius Vanderbilt once realized he had been cheated by two of his partners, Charles Morgan and C. K. Garrison, so he sent them the following letter: "You have cheated me. I won't sue you, the law is too slow. I will ruin you."

Linda Ronstadt

Performer Linda Ronstadt is the granddaughter of prolific inventor Lloyd Groff Copeman. Copeman earned a fortune through his inventions, which included the rubber ice cube tray, a tamperproof envelope, and the grease gun. He also invented the electric stove, founded the Copeman Electric Stove Company, and sold it in 1918 to Westinghouse for a small fortune. The rubber ice cube tray earned him more than half a million dollars in profit before he sold it to General Motors. Only two weeks before his death, he was granted a patent for a beer dispenser and cooler.

Ann Sothern

Actress Ann Sothern is the granddaughter of Simon Lake, credited by history as the inventor of the submarine. Simon came from an innovative family: his grandfather, also named Simon Lake, was the founder of Ocean City, New Jersey, and his father, John Christopher Lake, was the inventor of shade rollers. When only twenty years old, Simon submitted his design for a submarine to the Navy Department, who summarily rejected it because he was so young and settled on the design of another company, whose submarine promptly went straight to the bottom. To prove the value of his design, Simon built his own prototype submarine, the *Argonaut Jr.*, and the Navy bought it.

Tuesday Weld

TUESDAY WELD

ELI WHITNEY

Actress Tuesday Weld is related to Eli Whitney, the inventor of the cotton gin. In 1792 after graduating from Yale, there being a lack of good jobs in the North, Eli went to Savannah, Georgia, where he became interested in the difficulty that planters had in removing the seeds from cotton. Eli was always handy with machines, having already created a needlework machine, and he immediately produced a cotton "engine." It was a huge success, so much so that people pirated his idea right and left, and the legal fees he spent protecting his invention sucked up all of his profits.

Peter Benchley

Authors Peter Benchley and Robert Benchley are related to Robert Goddard, a pioneer in space travel. Robert Goddard had a revelation when he was 17, in which he imagined that he was going to fly to the moon in a space ship. Every year after that, he would visit the tree where he had the vision. Unfortunately, when he published his book on the subject, *A Method of Reaching Extreme Altitudes*, it got him labeled "moon man" instead of gaining him the respect of the scientific community. He had the last laugh; today he is recognized as a pioneer of space flight.

Carole Lombard

Actress Carole Lombard, the wife of actor Clark Gable, was the great-granddaughter of Gentleman Jim Cheney, friend and confidential advisor to robber baron Jay Gould. Whenever Jay Gould made money, Cheney added to his own personal fortune. Among other financial ventures, Cheney was involved in laying the first transatlantic cable, and held several patents.

CAROLE LOMBARD

Olivia Newton-John

Singer and actress Olivia Newton-John's maternal grandfather was German physicist Max Born. He received the Nobel Prize in physics in 1954 for his groundbreaking work in modern atomic theory, including quantum mechanics, which ultimately led to the development of the atomic bomb. He said of his world-famous breakthrough, "I just remembered a little algebra from school, and a few simple theorems about matrices. But that sufficed. A little playing around with Heisenberg's physical formula showed the connection."

Barbara Eden

Actress Barbara Eden is related to Benjamin Franklin, who was not only a revolutionary, but also a scientist who invented the Franklin stove, bifocal glasses, and a glass harmonica for which Wolfgang Amadeus Mozart wrote musical scores. His discovery, with a kite, a string, and a key, that lightning is electricity led to his invention of the lightning rod. Benjamin Franklin was an authentic American genius, but he wasn't above using his ideas for less sophisticated uses. He created a party game in which people rubbed electrically charged rods for a thrill. Once, Franklin was walking with friends near a small pond when the wind began to blow, making waves on the water. Announcing he could calm the waves, he held his stick over them and the water became flat. They were amazed. What they didn't know was that he had dropped oil onto the water from a hole in his hollow bamboo cane.

Spencer Tracy

SPENCER TRACY

Academy award-winning actor Spencer Tracy was descended from Nicholas Brown, the founder of Brown University. The Brown family had been in Providence, Rhode Island, since the early days when they arrived in the colony with founder Roger Williams. They purchased vast tracts of land from the Indians, and the family still lived there a century later when they built Brown University on that same land. Not only did Nicholas Brown donate the land on which the school stands, but, being a wealthy and prosperous merchant, he also built all of the original buildings and heavily endowed the school.

NICHOLAS BROWN

Marlene Dietrich

Actress Marlene Dietrich's maternal grandfather was Conrad Felsing, heir to the Felsing Jewelry Company, which had been founded by her great-great-grandfather. Her father was Major Louis Dietrich, an officer in the German army in the years before World War I, when the cavalry still carried lances. Because her voice was so unique, Dietrich was often asked if she objected to being imitated by other actresses. Her reply was simple: "Only if they do it badly."

Franklin D. Roosevelt

President Franklin Delano Roosevelt is the grandson of one of the biggest drug dealers of the nineteenth century. His grandfather Warren Delano founded the family fortune smuggling opium from Turkey into China. This was a very profitable business; by 1835 there were over two million Chinese addicted to the drug, and more being born every day. The Chinese government tried to stop the trade, even capturing Delano during the Opium Wars, but nothing could stop it. Delano's huge fortune placed his descendants very much at the top of society, but the family tried to downplay the source of their wealth. However, in 1953, when Eleanor Roosevelt visited Hong Kong, she did some investigating and was forced to admit the truth.

Fourteen

POLITICIANS

Politics is a lot like show business. Your primary job is providing daily entertainment to the masses. It's not surprising that those who were popular enough to get elected might have relatives popular enough to make it in show biz.

Tallulah Bankhead	≋	Congressman William Brockman Bankhead
Lon Chaney	≋	Congressman Chaney
Bo Derek	≋	William Clayton, Colonial Governor of Pennsylvania
Ralph Edwards	≋	John Cummins Edwards, Governor of Missouri
Kiefer Sutherland	≋	Thomas Clement Douglas, Premier of Saskatchewan
Angela Lansbury	≋	George Lansbury, Prime Minister of England
Raymond Massey	≋	Vincent Massey, Prime Minister of Canada
Rudyard Kipling	≋	Stanley Baldwin, Prime Minister of England
Olivia de Havilland and Joan Fontaine	≋	William Pitt, Prime Minister of England

109

Helena Bonham-Carter	≋	Herbert Asquith, Prime Minister of England
Maclean Stevenson	≋	Adlai Stevenson
Tuesday Weld	≋	William Floyd Weld, Governor of Massachusetts
Sophia Loren	≋	Benito Mussolini
George S. Patton	≋	Benjamin Davis Wilson, Mayor of Los Angeles
Cecil B. De Mille	≋	Sir Herbert Louis Samuel, First High Commissioner of Palestine

Kiefer Sutherland

Actor Kiefer Sutherland is the son of actor Donald Sutherland and stage actress Shirley Douglas. He is the grandson of Thomas Clement Douglas, who for over twenty years was premier of Saskatchewan, Canada, and who is considered the architect of Canadian socialism.

Olivia de Havilland and Joan Fontaine

The de Havilland family has given rise to a number of notable descendants including actresses Joan Fontaine and Olivia de Havilland. (They are both de Havillands, Joan came into show business later and didn't want to be confused with her sister.) The founders of the de Havilland Aircraft Company, famous for its fighter aircraft that helped win the Battle of Britain during World War II, are first cousins to the famous de Havilland sisters. Their aircraft included the Tiger Moth, Gypsy Moth, Vampire, Mosquito, Albatross, and the Comet, the world's first jet airliner.

An even more illustrious connection for the de Havillands is their relationship to two famous prime ministers of England. William Pitt, earl of Chatham, is chiefly remembered as the prime minister after whom Pittsburgh is named. When the English took Fort Duquesne from the French during the Seven Years' War, they renamed it Fort Pitt in his honor. His son, called William Pitt the Younger, was the youngest prime minister in British history at age 24. He took power in 1783 and was able to accomplish what his father could not: he made peace with America, which gave the United States complete independence.

Helena Bonham-Carter

Actress Helena Bonham-Carter's great-grandfather was the Liberal prime minister Herbert Asquith. He will always be remembered as the man who introduced the phrase "wait and see" into the English language. She is also the granddaughter of Lady Violet Asquith, the grand old lady of English politics, a famous voice on early radio and a supporter of women's rights. Violet once asked her stepmother, Margot, if she planned to wear her favorite hat to Lord Kitchener's funeral. Margot replied, "How can you ask me? Kitchener saw me in that hat twice!" Margot Asquith, who was the second wife of Lord Herbert Henry Asquith and the mother of film director Anthony Asquith, once met Jean Harlow, who pronounced her first name as if it rhymed with "rot." Lady Asquith corrected her: "My dear, the 't' is silent, as in Harlow."

Angela Lansbury

Actress Angela Lansbury's grandfather George Lansbury was a radical leader of the British Labour party during the depression. When he was first elected to Parliament in 1910, he was asked to resign because of his radical support of women's rights. George was also a pacifist, a friend of Indian leader Mahatma Gandhi, and even resigned from his beloved Labour party in 1935 when it voted to support the League of Nations, because the League advocated war as a manner of enforcing policy. Even today, as famous as Angela Lansbury has become as an actress, she is still referred to in England as the granddaughter of George Lansbury.

Raymond Massey

RAYMOND MASSEY

Actor Raymond Massey was the brother of Vincent Massey, the first Canadian-born prime minister of Canada, and they were the grandsons of Hart Almerrin Massey, manufacturer of Massey-Ferguson farm machinery. Their immigrant ancestor was Geoffrey Massey, who sailed in 1629 from Bristol, England, on the ship *Lyon*, part of the great fleet that accompanied Governor John Winthrop, often called the Winthrop Fleet, and who settled in Salem, Massachusetts. Even though Raymond Massey's ancestor Jonathan Massey served as a Revolutionary soldier, Jonathan's son Daniel moved to Ontario, Canada, and served with the British in the War of 1812, fighting against the United States.

Rudyard Kipling

Author Rudyard Kipling based his writing on his experiences as a journalist in India in the 1880s, and in 1907 he was awarded the Nobel Prize for literature. His work has been made into many films, including *Gunga Din*, *Wee Willie Winkie*, *The Jungle Book*, *Kim*, and *The Man Who Would Be King*. Kipling's first cousin, Stanley Baldwin, was prime minister when Edward VIII decided to abdicate the throne of England in order to marry Mrs. Wallis Simpson. She wasn't considered queen material because she was an American citizen of illegitimate birth who had divorced one husband and was on the eve of divorcing the second.

Even though his books are action-adventure, Kipling had quite a sense of humor. Surprised to read his obituary in a newspaper, he wrote to the paper, declaring, "I've just read that I am dead. Don't forget to delete me from your list of subscribers."

Ralph Edwards

RALPH EDWARDS

Ralph Edwards, who created the hit TV series *This Is Your Life*, is the grandson of John Cummins Edwards, who was elected governor of Missouri during the Mexican War. Governor Edwards personally helped raise troops for the invasion of Mexico, being an advocate of manifest destiny, the theory that advocated expansion of the United States all the way to the Pacific Ocean. Rather than sit on his laurels in Missouri, Edwards joined the California gold rush when his term was up. His departure from politics was short-lived, however. There wasn't any law west of the Pecos, and as the owner of a

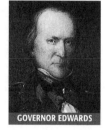

GOVERNOR EDWARDS

successful supply store for miners in Stockton, California, he needed some law and order. Edwards ran for mayor, won, and started hanging marauders right and left. Close to 50 years old, Edwards bought a cattle ranch, married, and settled down to a life of domestic tranquility.

Tallulah Bankhead

Actress Tallulah Bankhead's father, William Brockman Bankhead, was a U.S. congressman and Speaker of the House. Once, when he checked into a hotel, the receptionist said, "You're not *the* Mr. Bankhead?" He answered, "Yes, I'm Congressman Bankhead." Her face fell. "Oh, I thought you were Tallulah's father."

TALLULAH BANKHEAD

Tallulah's grandfather, senator John Hollis Bankhead, was wounded three times during the Civil War. When the senate refused to appropriate money for a statue of Robert E. Lee, John wore his Confederate uniform every day until they changed their minds. His largest project in the Senate resulted in the authorization of a federal transcontinental road, the Bankhead Highway, which ran from Washington, D.C., to the Golden Gate Bridge. When he died, he was the oldest living Confederate veteran in the U.S. Senate.

Maclean Stevenson

Maclean Stevenson, star of TV's *M*A*S*H*, claims as a relative Adlai E. Stevenson, Grover Cleveland's vice president, whose major claim to fame was that he was the grandfather of the more famous Adlai Stevenson who ran twice against Eisenhower. When the more recent Stevenson ran for president, one of his enthusiastic fans declared, "Every *thinking* person will be voting for you." Stevenson looked squarely at the woman, and said, "Madam, that is not enough. I need a majority."

Bo Derek

Actress Bo Derek is a direct descendant of Robert de Clayton, who was born in Caudebec, Normandy, and who served with William the Conqueror at the Battle of Hastings. In return for this service, he was made Lord of the Manor of Clayton. A more immediate ancestor was William Clayton, who was born in Yorkshire in 1625 and who became governor of Pennsylvania in 1683.

Sophia Loren

Actress Sophia Loren is genealogically connected to Italian premier Benito Mussolini through her sister, who married his son. Sophia is the godmother of her sister's daughter, actress Alessandra Mussolini. An amusing incident occurred when Peter Ustinov was visiting Sophia and her sister Maria. Baby Alessandra crawled out on the balcony. "For God's sake!" Ustinov exclaimed. "Don't let her go out there!" "It's quite safe," replied Sophia. "It's not that," Ustinov said, "but that's just how her grandfather [Benito Mussolini] started, crawling out on balconies, and look what happened to him!"

General George S. Patton

General George S. Patton's grandfather, Benjamin Davis Wilson, was mayor of Los Angeles and managed to name a few local landmarks as a result. Wilson was one of the first Americans to arrive in southern California, and he acquired extensive land holdings by his marriage to Ramona Yorba, the daughter of one of the old rancho families. His donation of land to the Southern Methodist Church resulted in the founding of Wilson College. Big Bear Lake in the San Bernardino Mountains got its name because that's where Wilson lassoed twenty-two bears. He also put his name on Mount Wilson, where he cut the first path up the mountain, and on which today stands the famous observatory.

Cecil B. De Mille

Film director Cecil B. De Mille is a cousin, through his mother, of Sir Herbert Louis Samuel, the first viscount Samuel and the first high commissioner for Palestine.

Fifteen

THE ALAMO

There are a number of famous celebrities who are justly proud of the fact that they are descended from one of the 180 defenders of the Alamo, all of whom were killed when the fort was overrun by the Mexican Army under General Antonio López de Santa Anna in 1836. The fall of the Alamo galvanized Texas like nothing could have. At San Jacinto, shouting "Remember the Alamo!" the Texans soundly defeated the Mexicans.

What happened to Santa Anna? He finally ended up in exile on Staten Island. He had brought with him a substance called chicle, which Mayan Indians had been chewing for centuries. At that time there was no gum in America, but Santa Anna's invention of chic-lets soon had all of New York snapping and chewing.

Hugh Downs ≋ Davy Crockett
Bowie Kuhn ≋ Jim Bowie
Audie Murphy
Gene Autry

Hugh Downs

HUGH DOWNS

Television newsman Hugh Downs has his own chart of his descent from Davy Crockett. Davy was already a national hero, frontiersman, and a former U.S. congressman when he entered San Antonio leading a company of Tennessee volunteers and died defending the Alamo.

When he lost his Congressional election in 1835, Davy declared, "My constituents can go to hell, and I will go to Texas." Unlike most of the defenders, he was not a Texan, but had just meandered into town looking for a good fight. He had previously picked up the title of "colonel" fighting Indians with Andrew Jackson, and he entered the Alamo leading a whole company of Tennessee militia. Extremely good at self-promotion, he published best-selling books about himself, set-

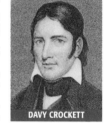

DAVY CROCKETT

ting off a Davy Crockett craze that lasted twenty years and wouldn't be equaled until Walt Disney started it all over again in the 1950s.

Bowie Kuhn

Former baseball commissioner Bowie Kuhn's first name memorializes the fact that he is a descendant of Alamo defender Jim Bowie, the inventor of the Bowie knife and one of the first men to volunteer to defend the Alamo.

Jim Bowie came from adventuresome stock; his father had served with Francis Marion, "the Swamp Fox," during the American Revolution, and had then married a girl he had plucked from a finishing school in Savannah. Once, when his father was jailed for shooting a trespasser, this young lady from the finishing school smuggled in a couple of pistols, and when they emerged together from the prison she was sighting down the barrel of one of them.

Jim Bowie used his famous Bowie knife to great effect in many a duel, and the newspapers couldn't get enough of his exploits. By the time of

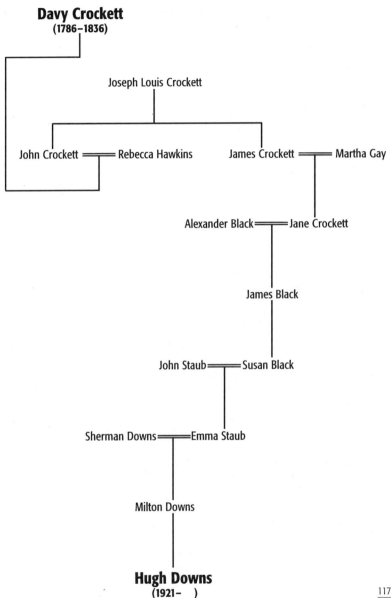

Davy Crockett
(1786–1836)

Joseph Louis Crockett

John Crockett ══ Rebecca Hawkins   James Crockett ══ Martha Gay

Alexander Black ══ Jane Crockett

James Black

John Staub ══ Susan Black

Sherman Downs ══ Emma Staub

Milton Downs

Hugh Downs
(1921–   )

LEO CARILLO

LEO CARILLO

Texas isn't the only state to join the Union after revolting from the oppressive yoke of Spanish and Mexican government. California followed the same road as Texas, under Hispanic leadership. Leaders of this movement were ancestors of Leo Carillo.

Actor Leo Carillo is most familiar for his role as Poncho in the television series *The Cisco Kid*. However, his background is among the most distinguished in California. He donated part of the vast landholdings which he inherited to the state of California, and today it is Leo Carillo State Beach in Los Angeles.

Leo Carillo's ancestor, Juan Bandini, issued a proclamation in 1831 renouncing his allegiance to the Spanish governor of California. Then he seized the Presidio in San Diego and imprisoned the officers. The governor sent an army to quash the rebels, and they met at the Battle of Cahuenga Pass, where Universal Studios stands today, and defeated the forces of the governor of California. Juan remained a revolutionary, and when John Charles Frémont liberated California during the Mexican War, Juan supported the annexation to the United States. His daughter, Maria, was reputed to be one of the most beautiful women in California and became known as the Betsy Ross of that state. She made by hand the first American flag to be raised over San Diego, which was raised on the arrival of Frémont. Her father-in-law, Carlos Carillo, another ancestor of Leo's, who had seized the government with his friend Juan Bandini, was proclaimed governor of California.

the Alamo he was as famous as the president himself. Whether it was a barroom fight, a duel, or his killing of John LaFitte, the son of the famous pirate, it all made good copy. He had his knife mass-produced in Sheffield, England, and no self-respecting frontiersman or riverboat pirate could be without one, because it was just as effective in skinning animals as in disemboweling an enemy. After the fall of the Alamo, Jim Bowie was found surrounded by the bodies of twenty dead enemy soldiers, his trusty knife in one of them.

Audie Murphy

War hero and film star Audie Murphy's great-grandfather was John Berry, a gunsmith. On his way to the Alamo, Davy Crockett stopped by to ask him to repair his famous gun "Old Betsy," which had a cracked stock. Berry placed a silver band on the gun to keep the stock from cracking further. After the Alamo, the Mexicans bragged that they had captured Cockett's "silver mounted rifle." When he heard what had happened at the Alamo, John Berry immediately volunteered for the army, and was with the Texas army when it defeated Santa Anna at the Battle of San Jacinto.

Gene Autry

GENE AUTRY

Singing cowboy Gene Autry's relative Micajah Autry was another defender of the Alamo. Attorney Micajah Autry was a friend of Davy Crockett in Tennessee, and when Davy suggested they take a ride down to Texas to help in the fight against Mexico, Autry went along. Autry thought that when the smoke cleared, they might make him the first attorney general of Texas.

Today, every year on the Saturday before the Fourth of July, Micajah Autry Day is celebrated in his home town of Autryville, North Carolina. A dramatic play of Micajah's life is acted out at an outdoor theater beginning at dusk.

Sixteen

CIVIL WAR HEROES

The Civil War (1861–1865) is by far the most significant period in American history. All other wars pale in comparison. More Americans died in the Civil War than in any other war. In fact, more Americans were killed in a single battle in the Civil War than died in all of Vietnam. It was the last war fought on American soil, and it was also the war that forged this nation into a single country. Before the Civil War, a person would say he was a "Virginian" or a "New Yorker." Afterwards, a new phrase was coined: "I am an American."

◎◎

Lee Marvin ≋	Robert E. Lee
Montgomery Clift ≋	General Robert Anderson, Commander of Fort Sumter
Happy Rockefeller ≋	General George G. Meade, Victor at Gettysburg
Julie Harris ≋	John Brown
Anjelica Huston ≋	General William Richardson
Roger Mudd ≋	Dr. Samuel Mudd
Margaret Sullavan ≋	Robert E. Lee
Helen Keller ≋	Robert E. Lee
Chevy Chase ≋	General Phillip Kearny

Lee Marvin

LEE MARVIN

Actor Lee Marvin received an Oscar for his portrayal of a drunken gunfighter in the 1965 film *Cat Ballou*. He always played the rough-and-ready, hard-hitting tough guy, without any trace of the southern aristocracy from which he had sprung. Although Lee Marvin has two lines of descent from the Washington family, his mother was clearly more impressed with her relationship to Confederate general Robert E. Lee. Or maybe she just thought "Lee" sounded better than "Washington Marvin."

LIGHT HORSE HARRY LEE

His relative, General Henry "Light Horse Harry" Lee, fought with George Washington in the Revolution, and he wrote and delivered the funeral oration for Washington before both houses of Congress, where he uttered these famous words: "First in war, first in peace, and first in the hearts of his countrymen."

Lee Marvin's relative Robert E. Lee is the reason that Arlington is now a national cemetery. It was his plantation before the war, and while Lee

ROBERT E. LEE

fought for the South, it was seized by the Union army. It was used first as a hospital and then as a cemetery, and by the end of the war, over sixteen thousand Union soldiers were buried on the plantation. After the war, the family struggled to regain the property. Finally, in 1882, the U.S. Supreme Court ruled that they were the rightful owners. However, since it was useless at that point for anything but a federal cemetery, Lee's son, Custis, agreed to sell it back to the government, and now it's known as Arlington National Cemetery.

Montgomery Clift

Actor Montgomery Clift's ancestors played a significant role in the Civil War. His ancestor Colonel Robert Anderson was the commander of Fort

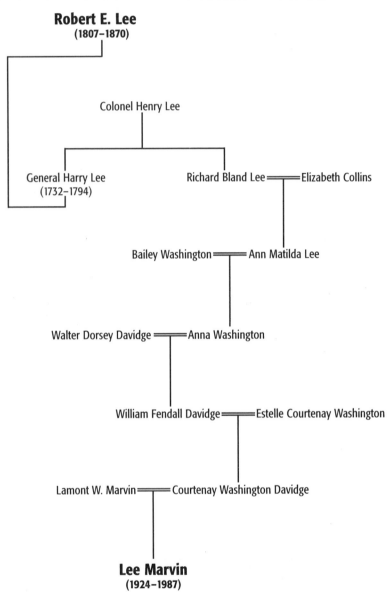

Robert E. Lee
(1807–1870)

Colonel Henry Lee

General Harry Lee
(1732–1794)

Richard Bland Lee ══ Elizabeth Collins

Bailey Washington ══ Ann Matilda Lee

Walter Dorsey Davidge ══ Anna Washington

William Fendall Davidge ══ Estelle Courtenay Washington

Lamont W. Marvin ══ Courtenay Washington Davidge

Lee Marvin
(1924–1987)

MONTGOMERY CLIFT

Sumter, which he defended against Confederate artillery until the buildings had burned, the main gate was destroyed, and the magazine was on fire. Finally accepting surrender on honorable terms, he marched out with colors flying and drums beating, saluting his own flag with fifty guns. A major general by the end of the war, he was sent to raise the Federal flag over Fort Sumter when the Confederacy surrendered.

A generation later, Colonel Anderson's wife, Elizabeth Anderson, refused to let her daughter marry Woodbury Blair, the son of cabinet member Montgomery Blair, even though her daughter was pregnant with Montgomery Clift's mother. Elizabeth was furious at Abraham Lincoln and his cabinet for not sending troops to support Fort Sumter. When Woody called her as mean as Mrs. Lincoln, he was banished from the house.

Montgomery Blair was not only in Lincoln's cabinet, but he was also a famous attorney, and their family home, Silver Springs, was one of the great estates of Maryland. Montgomery was the attorney for Dred Scott and argued for Scott's freedom based upon the fact that Scott had been living in a state where slavery was forbidden. The Supreme Court found against him in 1857, stating that a black slave could not become a citizen under the U.S. Constitution. Seen by abolitionists as a pro-slavery decision, the verdict was

MONTGOMERY BLAIR

one of the immediate causes of the Civil War. Always on the side of abolition, Montgomery Blair was later the defense attorney for John Brown at Harpers Ferry.

Happy Rockefeller

Happy Rockefeller is not only the wife of Nelson Rockefeller, former vice president of the United States and himself a descendant of oil magnate John D. Rockefeller, but she is also the great-great-granddaughter of General George G. Meade, the Union general who won the battle at Gettysburg.

The battle of Gettysburg was the greatest battle ever fought on American soil. The war until that time had been fought in the South, but it was Robert E. Lee's plan to make a thrust into the North in the hopes of forcing the Union to sue for peace. For three days the largest armies ever amassed in America were caught up in a frenzied battle. Finally, in an attempt to break the deadlock, George Pickett made his famous charge which resulted in the annihilation of his entire division. His army broken, General Lee was forced to retreat back to the South. Although the war continued for another two years, the South never recovered from this defeat, and the battle of Gettysburg is considered the high-water mark of the Confederacy.

Julie Harris

JULIE HARRIS

Actress Julie Harris is related to John Brown, one of the chief catalysts of the Civil War. John Brown decided that the only way to free blacks was by taking bands of armed men into the slave territories. He thought that one big push could incite all of the slaves in the South, and for this he needed a major supply of weapons. His plan was to seize all of the guns and ammunition stored at the federal arsenal at Harpers Ferry and then raise a huge army dedicated to freeing the slaves. He easily took the town, but was unable to hold it against a

JOHN BROWN

detachment of federal troops under the command of Colonel Robert E. Lee. Captured, he was tried and hanged for conspiring with slaves to rebel, a capital crime under Virginia law.

Roger Mudd

News commentator Roger Mudd was active in obtaining a pardon for his relative, Dr. Samuel Mudd. Dr. Mudd had been imprisoned for participation in the Lincoln assassination, a result of which the phrase "Your name is Mudd" was coined. With the help of Presidents Carter and Reagan, Dr. Mudd's case was reviewed by the army, who determined he was innocent, and he received a full pardon.

When John Wilkes Booth shot Abraham Lincoln at Ford's Theatre, his leg was broken when he leapt from the balcony onto the stage below. Seeking medical attention, Booth stopped at the home of Dr. Samuel Mudd. The good doctor set his leg, not knowing who he was, much less what he had done. When Booth was shot during his capture eleven days later, Dr. Mudd's best witness to his innocence died. Believed part of the conspiracy to kill Lincoln, Mudd was convicted in a military trial and sent to a hellhole of a prison in the Florida Keys. Films based on this unusual story include *The Ordeal of Dr. Mudd*, with Dennis Weaver, and *The Prisoner of Shark Island*, directed by John Ford, with Harry Carey and John Carradine.

Noteworthy: Even more amazing than the connection between the two men whose "name is Mudd" is the connection between Dr. Samuel Mudd and the assassinated president, Abraham Lincoln. The president was the nephew of Mordecai Lincoln, whose wife, Mary Mudd, was a cousin to Samuel Mudd.

Douglas Fairbanks and Douglas Fairbanks Jr.

Silent screen legend Douglas Fairbanks's father, Captain Hezekiah Ulman, was wounded at Bull Run, and thereby became a guard for President Lincoln at the White House. He was so handsome that he was often mistaken for the great actor Edwin Booth, who was the brother of Lincoln's assassin, John Wilkes Booth. Returning to civilian life, he became a lawyer, and went on to found the American Bar Association.

Actor Douglas Fairbanks Jr.'s maternal great-grandfather was Colonel David M. Thompson, the self-proclaimed Cotton King. Thompson had been a colonel in the Civil War, was captured, and later escaped from the infamous Confederate prison camp at Andersonville, Georgia. He made his fortune in cotton after introducing the cotton gin into New England. His company, D. B. R. Knight Cotton Mills, became famous as makers of Fruit of the Loom underwear.

W. C. Fields

W. C. Fields always protested that he didn't have any ancestors. However, his father, who was born in England, had enlisted in the Union army during the Civil War and was wounded in action.

Field's attitude towards family was exemplified by his response when asked if he liked children: "Of course, if they are served parboiled." When asked to clarify his answer, he replied, "Children? I like children. Girl children, between the ages of 18 and 21."

D. W. Griffith

Film director D. W. Griffith, the creator of the cinema Civil War classic *The Birth of a Nation*, inherited the southern outlook portrayed in those films. His father, Colonel Jacob Wark Griffith, received the last field promotion to general in the Confederate Army, directly from the hands of no less a personage than Jefferson Davis himself, the president of the Confederacy, when he helped Davis hide from the advancing Union troops.

Steve McQueen

Actor Steve McQueen's great-great-grandfather Pike Montgomery Thomson was a colonel in the Confederate Army. The Thomsons had fought in every American war from the Revolution through the Civil War. Pike's son, John William Thomson, was with Shelby's Brigade and fought at Independence, Westport, Little Blue, and Fayetteville, Arkansas, before the brigade marched into Texas.

STEVE McQUEEN

Jimmy Stewart

JIMMY STEWART

Actor Jimmy Stewart was descended from Samuel Getty, the founder of Gettysburg, Pennsylvania, the site of the most important battle in American history. On those hot and humid days in 1863, the hopes of the Confederacy were dashed, and one nation, the United States, was forged in blood. Both of Jimmy's grandfathers, James M. Stewart (his namesake) and Colonel Samuel M. Jackson, fought for the Union, and after the war Colonel Jackson was elected treasurer of the commonwealth of Pennsylvania. Jimmy came from a long military tradition in America, extending back to the Revolution, and he himself served in World War II, where as a pilot he flew more than twenty bombing missions over Germany and later rose to the rank of brigadier general. Jimmy's father, Alexander Stewart, walked out of a class at Princeton to enlist in the Spanish-American War and later served as a captain in World War I.

Margaret Sullavan

Through her parents, wealthy stockbroker Cornelius Hancock Sullavan and the socialite Garland Council, Margaret Sullavan, popular actress of the 1930s and 1940s, was connected to almost the entire Revolutionary and Civil War aristocracy of Virginia, including Robert E. Lee himself.

MARGARET SULLAVAN

Chevy Chase

CHEVY CHASE

Comedian Chevy Chase is descended from General Philip Kearny, a fiery warrior of the Civil War—and a bit of a wit himself. In the Mexican War, Philip Kearny led a remarkable cavalry charge at Churubusco that won the battle but in which he lost his left arm. Later, as a general in the Civil War, he remarked when he met a Confederate general who had lost his right arm, "We should buy gloves together."

GENERAL PHILIP KEARNY

Seventeen

SHORT TAKES

◉◉

You Might Not Know

John Wayne ≋	Winston Churchill
Diane Ladd ≋	Tennessee Williams
Oprah Winfrey ≋	Elvis Presley
Macaulay Culkin ≋	Bonnie Bedelia
Drew Barrymore ≋	John Barrymore
Glenn Close ≋	Brooke Shields
Francis Ford Coppola ≋	Nicolas Cage
Rebecca De Mornay ≋	Wally George
Morton Downey Jr. ≋	Barbara Bennett
Mia Farrow ≋	Maureen O'Sullivan
Melanie Griffith ≋	Tippi Hedren
Katherine Hepburn ≋	Katherine Houghton
William Katt ≋	Barbara Hale
Jennifer Jason Leigh ≋	Vic Morrow
Leslie Nielsen ≋	Jean Hersholt
Catherine Oxenberg ≋	Prince Charles
Ginger Rogers ≋	Rita Hayworth
Dinah Shore ≋	Ed Koch
Carly Simon ≋	Simon and Schuster
Sissy Spacek ≋	Rip Torn
Robert Wagner ≋	Katie Wagner
Mel Gibson ≋	Eva Mylott

Bud Abbott

William "Bud" Abbott, the straight half of the comedy team Abbott and Costello, came from a theatrical family. His father, Harry Abbott, was an advance man for P.T. Barnum's circus. Harry would go ahead of the circus, posting bills all over the next town to advertise its impending arrival. Bud's mother, Rae Fisher, was a bareback rider in the show. Bud Abbott and Lou Costello once took out a $100,000 insurance policy with Lloyds of London that paid off if anyone in their audience died of laughter.

Anne Baxter

ANNE BAXTER

FRANK LLOYD WRIGHT

Oscar-winning actress Anne Baxter is the granddaughter of architect Frank Lloyd Wright, who got her start in show business when he designed a theater for her when she was only three years old. She said of her grandfather, "I had a marvelous relationship with him. It was absolutely flawless." In 1959 she hosted a PBS special on her famous grandfather. Frank visited the set when Anne Baxter was filming *A Royal Scandal* with Tallulah Bankhead, who heard him remark, "Not bad for an old dame." In the next scene, Tallulah gave Anne a sock that sent her flying across the soundstage and out the door.

Mia Farrow

MIA FARROW

MAUREEN O'SULLIVAN

Mia Farrow is the daughter of film director John Farrow and Maureen O'Sullivan, who played Jane opposite Johnny Weissmuller in the Tarzan films. Both Mia's parents had very similar backgrounds. Maureen O'Sullivan's father was a major with the Connaught Rangers of Ireland and was wounded in World War I. John Farrow's father, Colonel Joseph Rashmere Villiers-Farrow, was a distinguished soldier who fought in the Indian and South African campaigns.

Errol Flynn

HMS *Bounty* mutineer Fletcher Christian has been played in the movies by Errol Flynn, Clark Gable, Marlon Brando, and Mel Gibson. However, the only one who actually descended from Christian was Errol Flynn. Flynn used his ancestral connection to get his first screen break in the 1933 Australian film *In the Wake of the Bounty*. He played his own ancestor, and he claimed his relationship helped him to get the role.

All of the films about the *Bounty* always end with their arrival on Pitcairn Island, but in fact Christian, after planting his seed in a race of South Sea islanders, returned to England, where he lived the remainder of his days under an assumed name as a country gentleman. There, he was recognized by Captain Peter Heywood, one of his fellow officers, but Heywood did not see fit, some twenty years after the crime, to turn in his old comrade to the authorities.

Rita Hayworth

RITA HAYWORTH

Actress Rita Hayworth's grandfather, Antonio Cansino, was the first in the family to enter show business. A professional dancer in Seville, Spain, he created Spanish dance as we know it today, combining Spanish classical dance with gypsy-based flamenco steps. His most famous dance was the bolero, which swept the world. His son, Eduardo Cansino, caught the attention of Mrs. Stuyvesant-Fish, the leader of New York society, and she brought him to America, where he instantly became a sensation, the darling of the social circuit. There he met a girl from the Ziegfeld Follies, Volga Haworth, and insisted that she give up her career when they were married, so she transferred her frustrated stage ambitions to her daughter Rita. In 1926 Eduardo Cansino opened a dance school in Hollywood, teaching the stars how to dance, and it was as a dancer that Rita first broke into show business.

Jerry Lee Lewis

Southerners use the expression "kissing cousins," but singer Jerry Lee Lewis and preacher Jimmy Swaggart's family has taken the idea to the extreme. Jimmy Swaggart's father, Willie Leon Swaggart, was the son of

Willie Harry Swaggart, but he was also his brother-in-law. This means that Elmo Lewis, father of Jerry Lee, was both an uncle and a brother-in-law to Willie Leon Swaggart. Therefore, Willie Harry Swaggart and Willie Leon Swaggart were brothers-in-law, uncle and nephew, and father and son, all at the same time. Minnie Bell Herron, who married Willie Leon Swaggart, was both the mother and the aunt of her son, Jimmy Swaggart. Both Jimmy Swaggart's mother and grandmother were also his aunts. That is because Jimmy's father and grandfather were brothers-in-law and uncle and nephew as well as father and son. All this confusion is probably one reason their grandmother Theresa Lee was institutionalized.

Ann Miller
Dancer and actress Ann Miller is the daughter of John Alfred Collier, a successful criminal lawyer whose clients included such notorious criminals as Baby Face Nelson and Bonnie and Clyde.

Helen Reddy
Singer Helen Reddy's fourth great-grandfather Richard Morgan of Bristol, England, was convicted of armed robbery and ended up on the first fleet of convict ships sent to Australia in 1788. Dispelling any theories about heredity versus environment, one of his descendants became an archbishop in the Church of England.

Jane Russell
Actress Jane Russell's great-great-grandfather Otto Reinhold Jacobi was a Prussian court painter and friend of William I of Prussia. His landscapes in watercolor are highly valued even today. He was commissioned to restore the Sistine Chapel in the middle 1800s. Otto was encouraged to emigrate to Canada by his friend the duke of Nassau, who was afraid that Otto's son Ernest would be drafted into the coming war. Otto opened a studio in Montreal and later in Toronto, and was one of the founding members of the Royal Canadian Academy, serving as its president from 1890 to 1893.

Kathleen Turner
Actress Kathleen Turner's father, Allen Richard Turner, was born in China, where his grandfather had been a Methodist missionary. Raised in China by his maiden aunts, Allen Turner was caught there when the Japanese occupied Shanghai during World War II, and he ended up spending four

years interned in a Japanese prisoner-of-war camp. This did not appear to sour him on foreign cultures, because he entered the Foreign Service and was the U.S. consul in Cuba when Castro came to power.

Mae West

Sexy comedienne Mae West, the star who invented sex in films, was never at a loss for a quotable, sexy line. In response to the question, "My goodness, where did you get those beautiful pearls?" her classic retort was, "Goodness had nothing to do with it." She liked the line so well that she used it as the title of her autobiography.

Mae claimed a connection to one of the great sex scandals of her day. She was a cousin to millionaire playboy Harry K. Thaw, who earned his niche in history by killing architect Stanford White for dallying with his wife, the former showgirl Evelyn Nesbit. This was later made into the movie *The Girl in the Red Velvet Swing*, with Joan Collins playing Nesbit.

Harry K. Thaw was rich beyond imagination and mad as a hatter. He regularly beat Evelyn and other women with whips. He constantly quizzed Evelyn about her affair with White, and she taunted him at every opportunity with graphic descriptions of their debauchery. Inflamed with jealousy, Thaw strode into Madison Square Garden, which White had designed, walked up to where he was dining with Evelyn, and proceeded to pump three bullets into him. Upon observing what he had done, Evelyn remarked, "You're in trouble now, Harry!"

The trial was sensational. White's own perversities were on parade: his private collection of pornographic photographs was displayed, including over 160 books of erotica. He also possessed at least a dozen volumes on flagellation, including *The Pleasures of Cruelty*. Evelyn described in minute detail her sexual escapades with both of them, and every newspaper in the country printed the transcript word for word. Judged insane, Thaw was thrown into a prison room that his interior decorators made into one of the most comfortable suites in the country. After five attempts at release, including an escape to Canada from which he was extradited back to New York City's Tombs Prison, he was finally declared sane and was released, whereupon he promptly divorced Evelyn.

ABOUT THE AUTHOR

Where Does The Author Find This Stuff?

Where does Mr. Davenport unearth these celebrity genealogical relationships? Some come from interviews with the celebrities, while others are the result of his own research. Often, a relative of a celebrity has more information than the celebrity himself. Other family connections come to him from professional and amateur genealogists across the country who know of his mania for collecting the roots of the rich and famous. And sometimes he just answers a request from a celebrity to look into his ancestry.

Clint Eastwood and Robert Davenport

CLINT EASTWOOD

ROBERT DAVENPORT

The most closely related Hollywood celebrity of the author Robert Davenport is Oscar-winning actor/director/producer Clint Eastwood. Clint Eastwood and Robert Davenport's immigrant progenitor, Richard Eastwood, was born in England in 1620 and settled in Portsmouth, Virginia. Their more recent relative is Asa Eastwood, who served as a sailor on the U.S.S. *Constitution*, an officer on a Dutch warship, and a chief of Tammany Hall. He held several political jobs, one of them being the thankless task of collecting the war taxes from Quakers in New York City. In 1821 he was elected a delegate to the New York State Constitutional Convention. He was originally a Democrat until 1856, when, opposed to slavery, he became a Republican.

In his diary, Asa wrote, "I have been a sailor, a soldier, a peddler, a rum seller, a hatter, a cartman, a copper, a farmer, a military officer, a civil officer, an office seeker, a merchant, a pettifogger, and a politician." He lived to be almost 90, and in response to questions about his longevity, he said the secret was diet and exercise, with total abstinence from snuff, tobacco, and whiskey. He was president of the Temperance Society, and when there was a heavy crop of grain in 1860, he commented, "Now the whiskey drinkers and tobacco chewers can live in beastly luxury." At age 89 he decided it was time to die, so he closed his business affairs and sent invitations to his old associates to be present at his funeral.

About Robert Davenport

Robert Davenport attended Middlebury College (B.A.), St. John's Law School (J.D.), Harvard Business School (M.B.A.), and UCLA Film School (M.F.A.). During Vietnam he was a naval flight officer, commanding a combat aircrew with Patrol Squadron Forty-Four, and during the Gulf War he was a captain in the U.S. Army. After law school he worked for the U.S. Department of Justice in Washington, D.C., and after business school he worked at various entertainment companies, including CBS, Viacom, New World, and Twentieth Century-Fox. His other published books include *Baby Names of the Rich and Famous*, *The Celebrity Almanac*, *Pet Names of the Rich and Famous*, *The Celebrity Birthday Book*, *The Davenport Genealogy*, and the *Hereditary Society Blue Book* (1st–6th editions). He currently makes his home in Los Angeles and works as a screenwriter.

Send Us Your Celebrity Genealogy!

Mr. Davenport welcomes any genealogical information on a celebrity that you would like to share, to be included in future books. Please indicate in your letter if you want to be listed on the acknowledgments page. Send your information to:

Robert R. Davenport
Roots of the Rich and Famous
Post Office Box 1989
Beverly Hills CA 90213-1989

INDEX

Page numbers in italics indicate illustrations.